SET APART

Devotions of God's
Steadfast Pursuit of You

COMPILED BY
DANIEL MCINTOSH

Harrison House
Tulsa, OK

13 12 11 10 09   10 9 8 7 6 5 4 3 2 1

Set Apart
Devotions of God's Steadfast Pursuit of You
ISBN 13: 978-1-57794-881-0
ISBN 10: 1-57794-881-5
Copyright © 2009 by Believers Church
4705 S. Memorial
Tulsa, OK 74145
www.bctulsa.com

Published by Harrison House Publishers
P.O. Box 35035
Tulsa, Oklahoma 74153
www.harrisonhouse.com

Contents

PERSONALLY CHOSEN

by Mark Steele

GOD *spoke to Moses: "See what I've done; I've personally chosen Bezalel son of Uri, son of Hur of the tribe of Judah. I've filled him with the Spirit of God, giving him skill and know-how and expertise in every kind of craft to create designs and work in gold, silver, and bronze; to cut and set gemstones; to carve wood—he's an all-around craftsman."*

Exodus 31:1-5 MESSAGE

Bezalel. Not the most household name. In truth, you've more-than-likely never heard of him before. Up until this verse, he was one of the hundreds of thousands of Israelites lost in the shuffle wandering in the wilderness. Bezalel had certainly heard of the great things God had done through specific men. Famous men. He would have heard how God had spoken through the mouth of Aaron and the rod of Moses. He would have seen the strong men fight like warriors and the gifted invent songs of praise. It is safe to assume that he would have classified these outstanding men as leaders, warriors, and romantics; and yet he would have never considered himself a candidate to share in their limelight.

Bezalel was committed to two things: the first was glorifying God and the second was his craft. He was talented and refined in the arts of woodcarving and working with precious materials. His patrons respected his close attention to detail and the guaranteed quality of his final product. His was a quiet, personal, solitary pursuit. The sort of pursuit that came in handy when making a living but was regarded by very few as godly. His craft was simply his means to survive—and he was very good at it.

What Bezalel had never taken the time to put together in his mind was the fact that God had created him to be skilled in these areas. He had literally been set apart—selected—to shine in an area where very few others had capabilities. Bezalel was committed to developing these God-given skills, but it is reasonable to assume that he would have never considered worshiping God with these gifts as another might in battle, in song, or in leading God's people.

The reason—Bezalel didn't know about the tabernacle.

God commanded Moses to instruct His people to make the House of God. Not *a* house of God, *the* House of God. It was to be the stunning monument by which all other gifts to God by man throughout history would be measured. The entire nation of Israel craved to be a part of this important construction, but when they volunteered their services, they were met with a resounding *no*. Only the ones set apart by God were to work on the tabernacle. Everyone else had only one responsibility–bring all their gold, silver, and jewels, and offer them as ingredients for

God's appointed crafters to turn into a work of art.

That set-apart someone was Bezalel.

Many times we attempt to be someone we are not, but when we do that, we are resisting what God has made us to be with the excuse that it doesn't seem as attractive as God's plan for someone else. But, God has given unique gifts to each of us for a reason: there will come a time and a place where that which makes you unique will be used powerfully by God. Bezalel was only ready to answer that call because he had accepted who God made him to be and refined the skill of his gifts with discipline.

> *Unique* works of God—*historic* works of God—can only happen through people who accept what sets them apart.

So many wander aimlessly because they never embrace who God made them to be. Instead, they attempt to be like a dozen others who seem to have the life or calling most desired. But, *unique* works of God—*historic* works of God—can only happen through people who accept what sets them apart and who work to refine their gifts so that when God comes calling, they are ready to act. People who realize the full definition of what God created them to be determine it is much better to accept God's path than to attempt to forge their own.

Slowly and steadily working with the gifts God has given us may not seem as glamorous as choosing our own paths, but in the end we will see how God's hand was working the entire time to reveal that we are each personally chosen.

HE STARTED IT

by Gyle Smith

Very rarely will anyone die for a righteous man, though for a good man someone might possibly dare to die. But God demonstrates his own love for us in this: While we were still sinners, Christ died for us.

Romans 5:7,8 NIV

Have you ever liked someone who didn't really like you? I have. I'm convinced that all of us are destined to have in our lives at least one person who, no matter how hard we try, we just cannot get it together around them. I knew a girl like this in college. She had everything I thought I could possibly want in a girl. Smart. Beautiful. Talented. Creative. All of those adjectives described me, too. Why wouldn't we end up with each other? It was destiny.

But somehow every time I tried to talk with her, what I thought was charming came out like the ranting of a crazed, and somehow at the same time miraculously boring, lunatic. I still can't figure out why she had this magical power over me that caused me to transform from a fairly average, nice guy, into a stuttering, drooling, slightly frightening, stalker-type guy.

And believe it or not, that's how I've often felt about God.

I've always known that I needed to have some kind of connection to God. I never really doubted that He existed, and I've always had enough fear of ghosts and death that I knew I didn't want to die without some relationship with Him. So I've pretty much always recognized that I needed to encounter God.

> To me, God was somebody who loved me just because it's His job to love everybody.

But when it came to actually encountering him, I struggled. To me, God was somebody who loved me just because it's His job to love everybody. I was just part of that general mix. For me to have a *relationship* with Him though—that meant I had to get my act together.

In other words, when I wanted to encounter God, it was all about me getting it right—praying right so that He would listen, acting right so that He would want to answer my prayers, and reading the right amount of Scripture.

But the problem was I could never really pull it off.

It was like trying to say the right thing to that girl in college. I'd prepare my speech, but it always came out spectacularly awkward. At times I didn't even want to have a relationship with God because I thought it would be too hard. I just knew I couldn't get it right. No matter how hard I would try to make God like me, He would always see me as a guy who was awkward and kind of embarrassing.

But then I found something in the Bible that fixed my screwed up view of God. You see, at just the right time, when we were still powerless, Christ died for the ungodly:

> *Very rarely will anyone die for a righteous man, though for a good man someone might possibly dare to die. But God demonstrates his own love for us in this: While we were still sinners, Christ died for us.*

Romans 5:7,8 NIV

Another version says it like this, "God put his love on the line for us by offering his Son in sacrificial death while we were of no use whatever to him" (Rom. 5:8 MESSAGE).

The point is this: God actually liked me first. All this time, I thought that if I could get Him to like me, then I could have a relationship with Him. But He started liking me before I had a chance to impress Him. In fact, He didn't start liking me because I had it together. He didn't start liking me because I was likeable. He liked me when I was "of no use whatever to him." He just liked me because He likes me.

This is the whole story of Jesus, "For God so loved the world that he gave his one and only Son, that whoever believes in him shall not perish but have eternal life" (John 3:16 NIV).

This verse doesn't say that God was so impressed with the world that He gave his Son. It doesn't say that He sent Jesus because He was so happy with the world. It doesn't say that the world was so cool and interesting. It says that He loved the world.

Our encounters with God are all about His initiative. We don't have encounters with God because we want them. We have encounters with God because *He* wants them. He is the one starting this relationship. He is coming after us. He actually likes us.

BE A GOOD CARPENTER

by Gyle Smith

And Jesus grew in wisdom and stature, and in favor with God and men.

Luke 2:52 NIV

"Where did this man get these things?" they asked. "What's this wisdom that has been given him, that he even does miracles! Isn't this the carpenter?"

Mark 6:2,3 NIV

I was an overachiever. (I say *was* because I think I'm almost over this illness. I'll be the best person to overcome it, EVER.) My school career was something I was proud of: 4.0 grade point average in high school and valedictorian of my class. Graduated college summa cum laude. Finished my master's degree with honors.

I was pretty confident that I had a good future in front of me. And I don't think I was cocky about it. I had worked my tail off to achieve what I did in school.

I'm smart, but I know there are people much smarter than I. I was just determined to work harder than everyone else. I think my motives were pretty decent. I really wanted to give God my best.

"Whatever you do, work at it with all your heart, as working for the Lord, not for men" (Col. 3:23 NIV), was a life mantra for me. I really sensed a "call" from God. I honestly felt that God had some kind of mission for me to accomplish. I was certain that God wanted to spend my life on something of eternal consequence, something that would leave a lasting legacy on planet Earth.

So, you can understand the confusion I felt during my first job right out of graduate school. With the applause of a grandiose graduation ceremony still ringing in my ears, I found myself in the only job that started paying the bills soon enough.

A file clerk. An insurance company file clerk.

I didn't study filing in college. Nor did I study insurance. I didn't even study business. I studied theology. Seven years. Two degrees. Cosmic ideas of serious significance occupied my mind day and night through undergraduate and graduate school. And now my life consisted of licking envelopes and shoving mounds of paper into endless file drawers, devoid of any possible meaning at all.

What happened?

My immediate interpretation was simple: Something had gone radically wrong. God had a call on my life. His plans for me were huge. I just knew it.

> The Man's job was to save the world, so He built chairs and tables.

There was no possible way that this job had anything to do with those plans. I hated it. It took every shred of energy I had just to drag myself into work each morning. And every day wore endlessly, grindingly on. How could this job have anything to do with God's plans for me?

But then it occurred to me that Jesus was a carpenter.

Jesus had a pretty important future. I don't suppose there are too many callings bigger than saving the world. That's a pretty important gig. And yet, for the greater portion of His life, something like 90 percent of it, He was doing something that seemed to have little or no relationship to His life mission. He was a carpenter. The Man's job was to save the world, so He built chairs and tables.

That made me feel a little better. Maybe there was something to the fact that I was working in a field completely unrelated to my life calling. Maybe my life was going like Jesus' did. Maybe those huge plans still would happen.

But then a really challenging thought occurred to me: What *kind* of carpenter was Jesus? Did Jesus drag Himself into the carpentry shop every day, sulking about the fact that He was doing such menial work compared to His life calling? Did He tell customers, "This really isn't my full-time gig. I'm actually here to save the world"? Did He do mediocre work? What kind of carpenter was Jesus?

The Scriptures don't really tell us what kind of carpenter Jesus was, but I'm pretty sure He was a good one. I bet that His clients loved talking to Him. And I'd guess that He was trustworthy. I would imagine that He got jobs done when He said He would, and if something delayed Him, He didn't make excuses. I bet Jesus was a great carpenter.

And so, my file clerk work took on new meaning. I wasn't just there on accident. I wasn't misplaced by God, waiting for Him to remember where He put me. God put me there on purpose. He wanted me to do my job well. Not just get it done but do it very well. I was supposed to be a great "carpenter."

Now I will say that after a long, humbling, and painful journey, I'm a pastor at a church. I love it. It's where I'm supposed to be. But, looking back, I wouldn't trade those days in the carpenter shop for anything. They not only prepared me for what I'm doing now, in a way they saved me because that was where I was supposed to be at that time.

Cherish your carpenter shop. God is working in you in deeper ways than you'll ever know. You're not forgotten. You're in the center of where He wants you. So be a good carpenter. You just never know what's next.

FLAWED

by Mark Steele

Confess your sins to each other and pray for each other so that you may be healed. The earnest prayer of a righteous person has great power and produces wonderful results.

James 5:16 NLT

When I was eleven, I was desperately afraid of all of my flaws. My parents, brothers, and friends had a certain image of me that deep down I knew was fraudulent. I believed that the best remedy for this fear was silence. Ironically, it was the silence itself that turned me into a fraud. The day I finally confessed my fears to those who trusted God and loved me, was the day that I began truly living and discovering the version of me that God had originally intended.

> **The enemy uses those failures to crush our confidence and keep us silent and alone.**

The enemy doesn't use our mistakes against us nearly as much as he uses the *fear* of our mistakes against us—the fear that others will find out how we failed.

The enemy uses those failures to crush our confidence and keep us silent and alone. This is the power of sin over our lives—to trick us into feeling that God's grace is out of bounds. But, the seat of despair we are buckled into has an ejection button: the power of confession.

We all know 1 John 1:9 NLT: "But if we confess our sins to [God] he is faithful and just to forgive us our sins and to cleanse us from all wickedness." We embrace this truth (as we should) because it is a confession that is not publicized. But, we are far more hesitant to live by James 5:16 because speaking that truth out loud to people will change things, and change doesn't feel very good at all.

When I confessed my sins and issues in a published memoir, it was difficult enough knowing that people I had never met now had a license to browse my anxieties over a latte. A far greater realization was that strangers would not be the only ones to read the book. Family. Friends. My church. So, I knew what I had to do. Part of my obligation to the truth was to stand up in front of my church on a Sunday morning and confess what I had done and how I was healing. So, I dry-heaved and obeyed.

An amazing thing happened. Unexpectedly, my confession did not put an exclamation point at the end of the sin, finalizing the chapter. Instead, it added a "but God" to the sentence listing my failures and ran on to a conclusion that healed others' lives and changed me. This is the real mystery of our flaws: we believe our sin will inevitably end us BUT GOD adds the miracle of confession to allow us to heal through one another. Somehow, in the nuances of God's plan, the power of the spoken word of truth breaks sin instead of sin breaking us.

A few days after the Sunday morning that I spoke, I received an email from a friend that said, "Sometimes I wish that that's what we did on Sunday mornings—just took turns getting up and being completely frank and open about where we are, where we have been, and how God brought us through."

Whether it's Sunday morning or Tuesday night, in front of a congregation or with your two closest friends at a coffee house, confession is how we prove that we trust God's promises are stronger than our fears. When we acknowledge we are flawed, while trusting that everyone else is as well, God breaks that prideful fraudulent wall down and breathes new life into the real you that was trembling behind.

SCAR TISSUE

by Adam Palmer

Therefore, if anyone is in Christ, he is a new creation; the old has gone, the new has come!

2 Corinthians 5:17 NIV

The older I get (just turned thirty; let's not talk about it), the more interested I become in baseball. I don't know if it's the slower pace of the game or all the stats or what, but I find myself drawn to the sport more than ever before in my life.

My new love of the game recently extended to the extreme dorkiness of actually following certain teams in the off-season and what their players were doing when they weren't playing the game.

Sad, I know. But bear with me—I'm going somewhere with this.

All this new interest in baseball led me to read a small item about the Houston Astros's first baseman, Lance Berkman, one of the principal sluggers for the team. He was hitting the ball well at the beginning of the season, and one of the main things he attributed it to was a procedure done to his knee in the off-season. His knee had been injured a few times, so he'd developed scar tissue.

> **God doesn't just chop out the bad bits of us; He takes those bad bits and makes them into new, good bits.**

In the off-season, he had his knee scoped and the scar tissue removed, and it greatly increased his athleticism and ability to knock homers out of the park.

When the body is injured, it does what it can to repair the damage, and that means scarring—places where the body reforms itself, but rigidly. In the case of Lance Berkman, it meant a loss of range of motion in his knee. Yes, he was healthy, but he wasn't the entire player he could be. For him, it was a simple matter of having the scar tissue removed in order to get back to top form.

No big deal, right? Except it got me thinking. How much scar tissue is around my heart?

Not actual scar tissue, mind you. I'm thinking of the emotional kind where someone hurt me, maybe really deeply, and I tried to mend the wound on my own. How many times have I been emotionally injured and scarred? How much scar tissue have I held on to keeping me from being the person I could be? How much scar tissue is preventing me from really loving like I should?

Ah, but there's good news in all of this because just like Mr. Berkman, I can have my scar tissue removed. In fact, God goes one better: God doesn't just chop out the bad bits of us; He takes those bad bits and makes them into new, good bits.

He transforms scar tissue into healthy tissue.

He makes me—and you—into a new creation.

That's the thing with scar tissue: it'll never be anything but a scar. But the beauty of God's plans and designs is that He doesn't just make the scars go away; He turns them into something we can use, a testimony of His goodness. Instead of those scars limiting us, they free us. They become a banner of God's love. They become signposts of His faithfulness.

They say, "Look what God has done."

You may not be a baseball player, but there's a good chance you have emotional scar tissue that God wants to mend. It is up to you to trust Him with the task.

HIDE AND SEEK

by Gyle Smith

Ask and it will be given to you; seek and you will find; knock and the door will be opened to you. For everyone who asks receives; he who seeks finds; and to him who knocks, the door will be opened.

Matthew 7:7,8 NIV

One of the earlier devos talked about the fact that God wants to encounter us. Our relationship with Him is really His idea. He thought of it first. It's God who started all of this but we have to make the decision to respond to Him. Just because He wants to encounter us, doesn't mean He's going to force us to do so. He actually wants to be liked back.

The Bible says this about Jesus coming to the world:

He came to his own people, but they didn't want him. But whoever did want him, who believed he was who he claimed and would do what he said, He made to be their true selves, their child-of-God selves.

John 1:11 MESSAGE

In other words, God started this all; but to encounter Him, we have to respond. In fact, God wants us to chase after Him a little bit. It's kind of like hide-and-seek. Jesus said it this way:

The game is rigged.

> *Ask and it will be given to you; seek and you will find; knock and the door will be opened to you. For everyone who asks receives; he who seeks finds; and to him who knocks, the door will be opened.*
>
> Matthew 7:7,8 NIV

God starts this relationship but, as one of my pastors once said, He sort of "hides." He waits to see what we will do. He wants us to come looking for Him. But here's the fun part: The game is rigged. He's like someone who is bad at hide-and-seek. He wants to be found.

I remember a time when my cousins and I were playing hide–and–seek at our grandma's house. I was the seeker. I came into the room where my cousin Russell, who was about six years old at the time, was hiding, and I found him lying on his back on my grandma's bed, head covered with a pillow. That was his hiding place. Somehow Russell actually believed that if he couldn't see me, then I couldn't see him. Russell was what we call a "bad hider."

And so is God.

He's a bad hider who really wants to be found.

So, here's the deal. God is the one who liked you first. He is the one starting up a relationship with you. He wants to encounter you. At the same time, He wants you to like Him back. He wants you to look for Him. The best news is God wants to be found.

If this is really true, and it is, you can approach God in a different way than you ever have before. You don't have to worry about being awkward; you don't have to get it all right. He just wants to be with you.

I'm from a family of all boys. My dad is from a family of all boys, and his dad is from a family of all boys. So knowledge about the opposite sex doesn't run very deep in our lineage. Not that it would matter much, I guess, because it seems that when a male is in the presence of a female he really likes, all useful intelligence evaporates.

My brother Andy is a great example of this phenomenon. Andy met Sara at a college Bible study and was quickly smitten. So, when the Bible study decided to have a barbecue at the park, Andy knew he had to make a move. He needed to get her attention and leave a lasting impression that would remove all doubt as to his date-worthiness.

When he arrived at the barbecue, from a distance he saw Sara engaged in casual conversation with a few other guys. This was his chance. Make the move he must. So Andy did what any red-blooded American male would do: He decided to be funny. Radically, side-splittingly funny. As he walked toward the group, he picked up the first stick he could find. He had decided that he would break this stick over his head in front of Sara and win from her a fit of uncontrollable laughter that could only lead to a happy and prosperous relationship.

Obviously a large deficiency in Andy's social awareness was exposed at this point, but even worse was the gap in his understanding of physics. Andy failed to notice that he had picked up a very short and very thick stick. So, as Andy powerfully and quickly slammed the stick down over his head, he heard what could only be described as a gunshot, followed by a high-pitched ringing that drowned out all other natural sounds around him. His teeth buzzed while pain stars floated in front of his eyes, and his knees buckled as he single-handedly came close to knocking himself unconscious—without breaking the stick.

Needless to say, the stick bit didn't win her over.

But then again, maybe it did. Sara is now his wife. Sara claims to this day that the stick incident wasn't the reason she decided to get to know Andy. In fact, I doubt the stick incident communicated anything close to what Andy had hoped. But Sara wasn't looking for a suave, debonair, social genius. She just liked him. She didn't care if he was cool or awkward. She didn't want him to perform for her. She just liked him, and that's exactly how Jesus feels about you.

BEING EXAMPLES

by Adam Palmer

Join with others in following my example, brothers, and take note of those who live according to the pattern we gave you.

Philippians 3:17 NIV

As iron sharpens iron, so one man sharpens another.

Proverbs 27:17 NIV

I am afraid.

I am very afraid.

Maybe not *afraid.* Maybe *unnerved* is a better word here. Or *unsettled.* A quick search of the in-computer thesaurus also suggests "frightened," "anxious," "nervous," and "panicky."

I am afraid/unnerved/unsettled/etc., because I am not entirely sure that God knows what He's doing when He says stuff like, "as one man sharpens another," and "join with others in following my example."

Surely He is not serious.

Right?

Please, God?

The more I think about it, the more I begin to realize, much to my dismay, that yes, God is serious about this—about us being examples to each other, about us sharpening one another.

And then I try to get out of it.

I do this for a variety of reasons but mainly just because of my own insecurities. Why on earth would anyone want to follow my example? I can be short with my wife. I holler at my kids about stupid things like the proper use of bathroom tissue. I drink too much soda. I don't exercise. I speed on the interstate (only five miles over, but still). I'm turning this devotion in late because I'm a horrible procrastinator.

The more I think about it, the longer that list becomes. I could spend my entire word count (and longer) pointing out all my flaws and foibles. But then I realize that maybe, just maybe, that's not what God is talking about here.

An example from my own life: my wife Michelle and I both love children. We love to be around them; we love to interact with them; and we especially love raising them. We have serious parental hearts. So when we first heard of the tiny orphanage Amani Baby Cottage that lies on the edge of Uganda, Africa, and that has connections to my church, our Parental Heart Meters leapt into action. We saw the pictures of the kids, we heard stories about the ministry opportunities, and we were stirred.

Individually.

We each thought that we needed to do something, but neither of us knew what the other one was thinking. I can't speak for her, but as far as I was concerned, I was ready to adopt the lot of them. When the logical side of my brain kicked in and protested to God, saying, "God, I want to do something, but we can't adopt *all* these kids," God promptly responded, "But you can adopt *one*, right?"

Uh…yes?

Uncertain, I mentioned it to Michelle, who, as it turns out, had been entertaining the same thought. So we contacted the orphanage, got the necessary info, and soon got the ball rolling to bring home Francis Sterling Palmer.

Here's where the *example* part kicks in. Michelle volunteers for an organization that helps adopt–out children born to women in crisis pregnancy situations. The director of the organization knows tons of potential adoptive families just waiting for babies, so Michelle mentioned Amani to her, and she made the orphanage an official option for any of those adoptive families. Already, families have started to take her up on the offer.

God does indeed know what He's doing.

There are now three more children being adopted from Amani Baby Cottage because of the example we set. We get calls all the time from those families, and other potential ones, asking about the process and what it entails. Maybe, eventually, our example can get all of those kids into loving homes.

The more I think about it, the more I begin to see that God does indeed know what He's doing. He isn't asking us to exhibit perfect behavior; He just wants us to listen to Him and to take a few cues from others who are doing the same thing. It's like Jesus said to the expert in the law after telling the story of the Good Samaritan: You see what that guy did, helping out his fellow man? You do it too. (Luke 10:37.)

A DIVINE GLIMPSE

by Jason Jackson

He who was seated on the throne said, "I am making everything new!" Then he said, "Write this down, for these words are trustworthy and true."

Revelation 21:5 NIV

On a beautiful Thanksgiving morning, Shagah Zakerion, a high school senior and student leader in our church's youth ministry, returned home after a four-month stay at St. Jude's Children's Hospital in Memphis, Tennessee. She had received a bone marrow transplant to treat a rare form of leukemia. Near baggage claim, a group from the church joined her family and close friends waiting for her return from Memphis.

For the most part, the mood was light. Frequent camera flashes illuminated a colorful mosaic of balloons and flowers held in jubilant expectation by the welcoming committee. Talk of Tennessee road trips and holiday entrees highlighted continual conversations whose lone and brief interruptions stemmed from glances toward the arrival board where Shagah's flight was labeled "on time." *On time* is good, but *arrived* is better. As we waited for the change, laughter abounded among the group with one exception. Shagah's father stood alone ten yards away from the rest of us. He stared incessantly down the long corridor while waiting restlessly for his daughter.

> Awe filled the terminal as father embraced daughter, tears running wildly down his face.

Many of us had been able to visit Shagah and her mom in Memphis, but her dad had stayed in Tulsa to run the family restaurant. I tried not to stare at him, but the longer I gazed, the more tangible his anxiety became. I wanted to understand, yet any connection I perceived was only a product of my feeble imagination. Four months of familial separation was not included in my list of life experiences.

I felt awkward about gawking, as anyone should, but my covert stalking techniques paid off. Just as no one else waited so anxiously, no one else celebrated so passionately when Mr. Zakerion's family emerged. Awe filled the terminal as father embraced daughter, tears running wildly down his face and a smile enlightened us all. Joy and relief united in an overwhelming chorus. Rarely in life have I witnessed such unbridled expression.

As I stood there looking like a paparazzi, I lowered my camera and considered removing my shoes because this ordinary airport had become a divine portico.

This reunion of family felt like a reunion of heaven and earth. In the book of Revelation, the ancient author John wrote,

> Then I saw a new heaven and a new earth, for the first heaven and the first earth had passed away, and there was no longer any sea. I saw the Holy City, the new Jerusalem, coming down out of heaven from God, prepared as a bride beautifully dressed for her husband. And I heard a loud voice from the throne saying, "Now the dwelling of God is with men, and he will live with them. They will be his people, and God himself will be with them and be their God. He will wipe every tear from their eyes. There will be no more death or mourning or crying or pain, for the old order of things has passed away."
>
> He who was seated on the throne said, "I am making everything new!" Then he said, "Write this down, for these words are trustworthy and true."
>
> Revelation 21:1-5 NIV

Imagine what it will be like that fateful day when heaven crashes into earth. The emotional Father welcoming His prodigals home. The joy pouring from each person's soul as they are reunited with loved ones. The parents who lost a child in their early years embracing their little one once again. The reunited husband and wife able to gaze into each other's eyes. The brothers and sisters who will dance with one another. And those who rediscover friends, joining together in celebration. I think about my friend whose teenage son died of leukemia and her face the moment of their reunion. I wonder how my mom, whose mother died shortly after I was born, will respond when she can be held in her mother's arms again.

When we are all reunited, we will also be restored. Those confined to wheelchairs will take their first steps. The blind will set their eyes on a sunset. The mute will speak and the deaf will hear their first song. Jesus will make all things new.

MEDITATIONS ON HAIR AND LOOMS

by Adam Palmer

> *Delilah then said to Samson, "Until now, you have been making a fool of me and lying to me. Tell me how you can be tied."*
>
> *He replied, "If you weave the seven braids of my head into the fabric on the loom and tighten it with the pin, I'll become as weak as any other man." So while he was sleeping, Delilah took the seven braids of his head, wove them into the fabric and tightened it with the pin.*
>
> Judges 16:13-14 NIV

It's interesting how many things you can learn about God when you boil the Bible down to its essence. My children have this Bible storybook written specifically for kids, and we read about three stories from it every night. Since it's written for kids, the stories are condensed to cover the high points.

When I read the story of Samson and get to the part where Delilah whines and complains to Samson to tell her the secret of his strength, Samson's varying answers read almost like bullet points:

- Tie me with seven fresh thongs (i.e. bowstrings) that haven't been dried.

- Tie me with seven new ropes.

- Weave my hair into a loom.

- Cut my hair.

(I think the Bible storybook people left out the "seven fresh thongs" for fear of confusing and frightening parents.)

> Samson was either clueless of Delilah's intent, or he was so sure of his greatness that he was toying with her.

Do you know this story, by the way? Samson is a strong guy, and the Philistines pay Delilah to love him up and trick him into giving away his secret. So she asks him about the secret to his strength, and he says to tie him with seven fresh thongs. He falls asleep, she ties him up, sends the Philistines in, and he busts loose and whoops some Philistine fanny.

Wash, rinse, repeat. Except this time, he says to tie him with seven new ropes.

Wash, rinse, repeat. Hair into the loom.

Get it?

Samson was either clueless of Delilah's intent, or he was so sure of his greatness that he was toying with her—attempting to have his sinful cake and eat it too, if you catch my meaning. My guess is the latter. I'm thinking that Samson was so impressed with himself that he was on to Delilah's ruse, but he was enjoying the, um, time spent with her, so he played along, each time thinking to himself, *How clever am I?*

He gets even more clever when he tells her to weave his hair into the loom because the secret to his strength really did lie in his hair, just not in the way he told her. I imagine that he chuckled to himself over that—how close Delilah really was and yet she had no idea.

I notice that I do the same thing. I say to myself, "Oh, I know that movie only has a couple of sex scenes in it, but I'll just fast-forward through them," or, "Man, that website has a lot of swear words on it, but it's just so funny!"

I'm hanging out with Delilah, and my hair is in the loom.

These things are skating close to the edge of sin. I may not be taking the full-on plunge into pornography or sailor speech, but man, I'm sure impressed with my ability to "retain" my holiness while participating in less-than-holy activities.

How clever am I?

I trick myself, more than I even realize. My hair is in the loom and the longer I keep tricking myself, the closer I get to the razor.

Take a moment to recognize the Delilahs in your life—activities that take you dangerously close to the edge. Don't fool yourself anymore. It's not only time to get your hair out of the loom; it's time to stop hanging out with Delilah.

NANOWRIMO

by Daniel McIntosh

Let's see how inventive we can be in encouraging love and helping out, not avoiding worshiping together as some do but spurring each other on, especially as we see the big Day approaching.

Hebrews 10:24,25 MESSAGE

"50,000 words in a month!"

A friend of mine was prompting me to believe that writing a novel in a month was a good idea. While I have bought into some hair-brained schemes in the past, writing a book in thirty days hasn't been one of them.

He gave me a book called *No Plot? No Problem!* to help evoke some quick novel-writing emotions inside of me. The author of this book is the founder of an annual happening called National Novel Writing Month or NaNoWriMo. Every November he organizes this irrational event when thousands of people begin writing 50,000 word fictional stories with the intent to finish before the month is over. Sounds outlandish, I know, but it has always been a goal of mine to write a novel, so I was intrigued.

> **Sometimes our best intentions are tripped up by sin. We need help.**

No Plot? No Problem! gives a step-by-step look on how to take your novel writing ambitions and turn them into reality. It includes several ingenious ideas on how to accomplish this task, and it says that the best way to ensure that you will complete your 50,000 word aspiration is to tell everyone you know that you are writing a novel in thirty days. Tell your friends, family members, coworkers—and tell them to tell people. Email people you haven't talked to in years, and tell them about your objective. Tell the lady behind you in line at the grocery story about your new endeavor. Tell everyone.

If everyone in your life knows that you are attempting to write a novel, then you won't be able to sweep it under the rug and act like it never happened when you get writer's block. People will be checking in on you. Friends will be asking you how your characters are coming along and what plot twists you are thinking about implementing. All of the sudden the thought of quitting is no longer an option because everyone knows that you're writing a novel.

The more I thought about this, the more I began to realize how this directly applies to our spiritual journeys. We need accountability. It is crucial for every believer to have that support system. We need friends asking us about our dreams and aspirations. We also need friends to help us in the midst of our struggles and temptations.

Paul addresses these struggles in Romans 7:17-21 MESSAGE:

> *If the power of sin within me keeps sabotaging my best intentions, I obviously need help! I realize that I don't have what it takes. I can will it, but I can't do it. I decide to do good, but I don't really do it; I decide not to do bad, but then I do it anyway. My decisions, such as they are, don't result in actions. Something has gone wrong deep within me and gets the better of me every time.*
>
> *It happens so regularly it's predictable. The moment I decide to do good, sin is there to trip me up.*

Sometimes our best intentions are tripped up by sin. We need help. We need someone to hold us accountable. Often times, it's a difficult thing to do. Sharing our shortcomings can make us feel uncomfortable but when we tell other people, it brings us into the light. And when we share our intentions, we are creating a strong defense against those temptations. Finding accountability in your life will help strengthen you and make you whole.

GOD'S DREAM FOR COMMUNITY

by Gyle Smith

The LORD God said, "It is not good for the man to be alone."

Genesis 2:18 NIV

I'm tempted to simply re-hash a sermon series here. You know, the one about how God wanted to hang out with people, but people kept blowing it. So God sent Jesus to take care of the whole obedience problem, and Jesus took the penalty for disobedience: death and separation from God. Then Jesus came back to life and invited us to hang out with God, and now God hangs out with us like never before—in us.

Now that's a pretty good devo to explain God's dream for community, right? I mean it pretty much summarizes the whole deal, but honestly, right now it doesn't really resonate with me. Now, don't misunderstand me—I think community is important. In fact, I think it's the most important thing there is. But now I have an understanding of community that I'm not sure I've ever had before.

You see, I've been alone for the last three weeks. I mean really alone. Like not being around humans much at all. And certainly not around any that I know. I'm in Virginia in an unfamiliar environment with unfamiliar people, taking classes to learn more about God. And I can't believe the cravings I have for community right now. It feels like my soul is a rubber band stretched too tightly. I want so badly to be with the people I love and who love me. And this has surprised me.

I tend to think of myself as pretty independent. Not super-social. I have to admit that I never have really understood the point of parties. How they serve any purpose for the greater good of humanity, I just can't see. (I think I just got uninvited to the next year's worth of get-togethers.) And I also have to admit that somewhere in the back of my head, I've always believed that if it were just God and me, everything would be all right. No. More than that. I thought that was it—just God and me. Sort of like my relationship with God is the conversation and everyone else is on call waiting.

I guess that has a little bit of truth to it. The God-and-I connection really is important. But I'm confident now that it's not the whole truth. Not even close. Because, guess what? I'm doing the alone thing with God like crazy, and something's still missing.

> Something deep inside of our collective gut hungers to love and be loved and just be...together.

You see, I'm praying every morning for at least an hour. And then I sit in a class for four hours and hear about God. And then I cloister myself in the library and study stuff about God for another four or five hours. And then, get this, I go home and pray a little more. And then I go back to the library and study stuff about God for two or three more hours. And then I go home and pray for awhile again and go to sleep only to get up the next day and do it all again. Every day.

You'd think by now I'd be a spiritual giant, able to predict the future and change the weather. But you know what I've found? I'm not. I'm just a scared little boy, simply wishing his family and his friends would be around to smile and say "hi." (As I'm writing this, I'm realizing how pitiful this sounds. The fact that a lot of people will be reading this when I'm in a saner frame of mind only increases my embarrassment. Oh well, I do have a point.)

You know why I believe it's God's dream for us to be in community both with Him and with each other? Because at the center of what it means to be human, something grasps for community, clings to anything that looks even sort of like it. Something deep inside of our collective gut hungers to love and be loved and just be…together.

Maybe this is because at the center of the universe God himself is community. You know, the whole one-God, three persons thing: Father, Son, Spirit. There are a lot of things I don't understand about God and this is one of them. But it's true. And it's beautiful.

Some theologians try to describe the Trinity like a dance; so much aliveness, movement, and interaction in God that even though there are three persons, there's just one essence; like incredible dancers artfully weaving in and out of each other. I love that idea, but I don't really understand it. I at least understand this: I think God's inviting us—together—into the dance. It's so good that He wants to share it with someone else, to have others know the joy of being together. To be community.

Maybe this is why Jesus spent so much time at parties.

TRUST

by Daniel McIntosh

Surely God is my salvation;
I will trust and not be afraid.
The LORD, the LORD, is my strength and my song;
he has become my salvation.

Isaiah 12:2 NIV

No one likes to get bad news. One example of bad news that I've had to deal with was when the worship pastor of our youth group announced he was leaving. I had just taken over as the youth pastor a few months prior to this news, and it sent me reeling. Thoughts of despair crept in during said reeling: *What horrible timing. I am not sure that the group can handle another leader leaving. This is going to kill us.*

A few days after the bad news and the reeling, the worship leader called me back and told me that he, his wife, and kids were not moving. The job that he thought that they had in Phoenix had fallen through. Well, this was great news! Not for him, of course, but it was great news for me. I was compassionate on the phone, but inside I was saying, *God You do provide! Well, not for him, but You do for me!*

About two months later, I went out to lunch with my fellow pastor, Gyle Smith. I told him about the roller coaster ride of emotions that I had been on with our worship pastor. Then I described to him how our junior high worship leader had recently led the music at summer camp for our youth group. During that week, I felt a strong peace that if our current worship leader was to leave, things would truly be fine. I told Gyle that I had a peace of mind about the whole situation. He looked back across the table at me and calmly said, "It's cool how God takes us on these journeys and gives us peace."

As we walked back up to the offices after lunch, my cell phone rang—it was the worship leader. He was calling to tell me that he had gotten another job in Phoenix. I listened to him on the phone as he told me how it would be hard to leave but that this was the right thing for him and his family.

I was taken aback at how the two conversations occurred within minutes of each other. I immediately went into Gyle's office and told him about the phone conversation and how the worship pastor really was leaving.

Gyle quickly responded, "Yeah, I know. He told me two days ago."

I stared at him before answering, "You knew? How could you not say anything as I was going on and on at lunch?"

> **Trust allows me to have closeness and intimacy with God.**

He said matter-of-factly, "It wasn't my place to say. It was his place to tell you."

True. It wasn't Gyle's place to say.

I walked out of his office with a huge sense of trust because I knew if I were in Gyle's position at lunch, I would have launched into how unbelievable this situation was and let the cat out of the bag. From this experience I learned that Gyle is a trustworthy guy. I knew that if I told him something personal about myself, it was not going to be broadcast to anyone else.

As I went back to my office, I had a realization about closeness and intimacy with God. I knew that because I could trust Gyle, it allowed for a closeness, even an intimacy, in our relationship. Trust leads to a closeness and intimacy. This human relationship helped me grasp how to have intimacy with a God I can't see, touch, smell, or taste. I have never sat down across the table from God and had a conversation, much less email correspondence with Him, but I have had numerous experiences (including the one listed above) that lets me know that I can trust Him. That trust allows me to have closeness and intimacy with God.

I know that God has been trustworthy. He has been faithful to me. He has proven Himself time and time again. He has remembered me. And those experiences of trust can lead me into intimacy with God. I can't see God with my eyes, but through this healthy human relationship, I am beginning to see how to put my trust in a God who has shown Himself trustworthy.

BACKSTORY

by Mark Steele

Standing on the barracks steps, Paul turned and held his arms up. A hush fell over the crowd as Paul began to speak. He spoke in Hebrew.

"My dear brothers and fathers, listen carefully to what I have to say before you jump to conclusions about me." When they heard him speaking Hebrew, they grew even quieter. No one wanted to miss a word of this.

Acts 21:40; 22:1-2 MESSAGE

Let's face it: the thought of revealing our deep dark secrets is enough to make the bile in our stomachs reach volcanic proportions. Whether intentionally or unintentionally, we spend the majority of our time playing the role of the poser: trying to paint a picture of ourselves to others that is much better than reality, and that disguises the stink underneath with cheap perfume. Somehow, we have been convinced that it is better to be

> We spend the majority of our time trying to paint a picture of ourselves that is much better than reality.

inaccurately considered perfect than it is to be honest and exposed as one who occasionally fails.

If anyone in history had reason to hide his backstory, it was certainly Paul. Paul had not only been living wrong, he had been murdering those who were living right. He had considered himself an enemy to all Christians. But, all of that changed on the road to Damascus in a radical conversion experience that left him temporarily blind as he realized that truly, he had been blinded in his old life.

Paul's story was ugly and filled with hatred. It must have been a very difficult story to expose. And, the truth is, Paul could have hidden the truth. He had, after all, changed his name. When the murdering in question was taking place, he was known as Saul. But as the light blinded him and the Voice spoke, the old Saul was blown to smithereens. All that was left was the new beginning called Paul. A fresh start. The opportunity to be known as something different. And yet, on several recorded occasions, Paul made a point to clarify exactly who he had been. He exposed his backstory and acknowledged that, yes, he had discovered a new beginning—but his old way had indeed been heinous.

In an era of "no publicity is bad publicity," we may not be surprised that someone of Paul's stature would step forward with his dark past. It might even have landed him a book deal with an option for movie rights. But, there was no benefit to Paul himself in exposing the story of Saul. And, this is exactly why Paul made certain the exposition took place.

We have all either been rescued from a dark place or are currently in mid-rescue. The twist the enemy throws into the mix is an attempt to convince us that it is best to keep that dark place a secret—that we could only be an effective picture of Christ if we deceive others into believing that we were, are, and always will be perfect. But, that is a lie.

Not only do we radically prove Christ is real by discussing our failings and allowing others in on our personal "before and after," but by speaking the hard truth, we also seal the deal. We give our testimony the power to continue to heal us, to continue to drive us toward Christ-likeness.

The enemy wants you to bury your demons because then you will someday forget them. And when you forget your demons, you are unprepared when they attempt to return. On the flip side, when we are willing to share our flawed selves, the remainder of the world realizes that they are not alone in their pain and that perhaps this Jesus they've heard about is real and can truly change their situation.

Paul realized this truth and was quick to upend others' impressions of him in order to radically improve their impression of Jesus. He revealed his own backstory so that they could see God's grand future for their own lives. There was indeed a cost involved: the cost of pride and of image. But the reward that awaited Paul—the same reward that awaits you and me—is the realization that though our backstories are flawed, in the telling, we are each made whole.

DIG DOWN DEEP

by Mark Steele

If you work the words into your life, you are like a smart carpenter who dug deep and laid the foundation of his house on bedrock. When the river burst its banks and crashed against the house, nothing could shake it; it was built to last. But if you just use my words in Bible studies and don't work them into your life, you are like a dumb carpenter who built a house but skipped the foundation. When the swollen river came crashing in, it collapsed like a house of cards. It was a total loss.

Luke 6:48,49 MESSAGE

When I was twenty-six, I had gallstones. Yes, that tiny word may sound insignificant, but the truth is that gallstones weave their way through your insides and cause staggering pain. Needless to say, I wanted them out, and I wanted them out quickly. My initial assumption was that there was something I could consume to dissolve them so that they could eventually make their way through my personal exit doors the way God intended. Unfortunately, this was not the case. In reality, my gall bladder would keep making bigger and badder upgrades of stones. The only true release would be to remove the gall bladder altogether—and that would require creating new exit doors in my body (i.e., surgery).

God says it is time for some serious surgery.

When we hear the words of Jesus in the parable of the house built on the rock, we like the way it sounds. Stability. Wisdom. Yes, these are good core principles that we are happy to implement into the current definition of our walk of life. But Jesus did not ask us to implement—He demanded that we uproot. The smart carpenter did not lay down a weighty and smooth stone on top of questionable ground. He did surgery on the ground itself, digging deep and removing roots and rocks—virtually creating a strong place to plant his cornerstone. Because He did this, the house withstood the rising waters of life.

We want Jesus. All of Him. But we have a tendency to add Him to whatever already stands in our lives. Instead of uprooting our lives and making Him the cornerstone, we try to implement holiness into all that is messed up, hoping that holiness will win the wrestling match. God says it is time for some serious surgery. He asks us to open wide and dig down deep, exposing our very nature—the sin and the wrong attitudes that linger long after our initial conversion experience.

This is painful—because whether or not we have fallen in love with our own wrongdoing, we have certainly grown used to it. Wrong motives become wrong words, wrong actions, and wrong habits. These are the very formula for a life built on the sand. Fortunately for us, God does not ask that we be the surgeons. That's His job. He does, however, ask us to be the ones to open up—to create the initial incision that exposes our lies and painfully wrong pursuits.

When my gall bladder surgery was all said and done, the incisions were barely noticeable; although, I did weigh considerably less and the harmful pain was gone. It had not been an easy road to travel. It was filled with introspection, discomfort, and an uncertainty of exactly what I would look like when the digging was over.

Similarly, in our own lives, we must allow God to burrow down to the very root of our behavior instead of stopping at the first moment of discomfort or guilt. A true cornerstone of Christ in our lives will lie underneath all else that is there, leaving no room for anything to hide down deep. It is time to expose our nature down to the marrow and allow Jesus to do some serious surgery.

RETELLING HIS STORY

by Mark Steele

Meanwhile, the eleven disciples were on their way to Galilee, headed for the mountain Jesus had set for their reunion. The moment they saw him they worshiped him. Some, though, held back, not sure about worship, about risking themselves totally.

Jesus, undeterred, went right ahead and gave his charge: "God authorized and commanded me to commission you: Go out and train everyone you meet, far and near, in this way of life, marking them by baptism in the threefold name: Father, Son, and Holy Spirit. Then instruct them in the practice of all I have commanded you. I'll be with you as you do this, day after day after day, right up to the end of the age."

Matthew 28:16-20 MESSAGE

I've known since I was a little boy that God gave me a mandate to spread His message, but I was constantly confused at what that was supposed to look like in my own life. The thought of opening my mouth and then being grilled about biblical truths was enough to give me the cold sweats. I loved stories, and I could sit at my manual typewriter for hours as a boy laying

> It appeared that God's perfect plan was only set aside for people who were the opposite of me.

them permanently to paper. But, opening my mouth? I had tried that, and only jokes fell out.

I don't know that I really had a full, accurate picture of what it meant to share God's story since all of my examples were extreme. There were the stories told by visiting missionaries who revealed how God would do miraculous things through my life if I would only sell my typewriter and move to a village where I would make my own clothing out of cornhusks and eat the parasites before they ate me.

Then, there were the Bible-thumpers who screamed with blood-red faces that God would use me only if I would decry all creative tools like art and music as strategies of the enemy of the Creator. This struck me as ironic, which made me laugh, which did not go over well with the thumpers.

The conflicting messages were enough to make me feel strange and different. Plus, it appeared that God's perfect plan was only set aside for people who were the opposite of me. Somehow, I had to sort through all of the messages and find out how to claw my way back to square one.

Then, I saw Jesus.

I had accepted Jesus a long time before that, and I knew all about Jesus for many, many years. But, one day as I was reading through the parables for the umpteenth time, I finally *saw* Him and the thought was revelatory.

He's doing what I like to do!

There Jesus was, standing in front of the masses, radically transforming their lives—through stories! He wasn't just saying, "Come be where I am," He was willing to say, "I will come to where you are." Jesus knew that His truth was *the* Truth but that it wouldn't matter a hill of beans if the people did not really see it—so He told the stories. He wrapped the truth in art. And as much as His methods mattered to me, what mattered more was the next realization.

He cares about MY story.

I wasn't weird or strange or the exception. Rather, I was built to be myself. Built to love and serve Jesus and to follow His mandate to lead others to Him—as myself. Yes, God wanted me to grow and become more like Him, but I was stuck trying to become more like everyone else. All along, in front of that typewriter, I was being constructed and shaped by Him to do the very thing I was afraid to do, and I was more than capable.

And this is the truest transformation: the realization that God built your story to tell His story. That for every unique creation, there is a fitting method of sharing His love, His truth, and His reality.

God needs us to be unique. He needs us to follow Him in unique ways. There are plenty of unique others out there who would follow Him, but they just don't see it. God designed you to be that someone who speaks their languages—and finally makes the Truth visible.

PRACTICALITY

by Daniel McIntosh

And the King will answer and say to them, "Assuredly, I say to you, inasmuch as you did it to one of the least of these My brethren, you did it to Me."

Matthew 25:40 NKJV

I experience a reoccurring inspiration every time I catch *Dead Poets Society* on cable. The epic speech by Robin Williams' character, Mr. Keating, challenges me to live life to the fullest. "Carpe diem," he tells his young pupils. "Seize the day, boys. Make your life extraordinary."

It's funny because no matter where I watch this movie or who I watch it with, I become so inspired by this scene that I make a personal commitment to myself (whispering under my breath) that I will "Carpe diem" from that moment on. I envision not wasting another moment watching TV or doing Sudoku. No, I choose to take life by the horns and seize every second of it.

Within about three or four hours, the inspiration wears off and I am back to watching a sitcom rerun. Why? What keeps us from

> **When we think about "going into all the world and preaching the gospel" we get that overwhelming feeling.**

taking this truth and inspiration from a teacher and putting it into our lives?

Practicality. The inspiration from Mr. Keating's speech is real, but the application is not there because seizing every moment is excessively hard to do. It's not practical, so we get overwhelmed and give up. It is so vast that it is hard to wrap our minds around how we can practically put this into our everyday lives. We need functional steps to help accomplish this enormous task.

At times, reaching out to our community can be an enormous task as well. When we think about "going into all the world and preaching the gospel" we get that same overwhelming feeling again. The vastness seems so great that we find it hard to stay as motivated as we would like and as the Scriptures call us to be. How do we rid ourselves of this lackluster performance?

Jesus gives a message to the disciples in Matthew 25 that helps us find continual motivation to take practical steps toward being an *outward* community. He also takes the blinders off of Peter and Co. as to what outreach means for them. Jesus tells His followers that when they clothe the naked, feed the hungry, and take in a stranger, it is as if they are doing it to Christ Himself. This gives them a real revelation of how much He values His followers' efforts to notice and help those in need around them.

When we think about reaching out to our community from that perspective, our passions rise, and it's easier to take steps to make outreach happen. We are able to view being mission-minded in a new light. The actions that we take here and now, and the things that we do to the least of these, not only make a big difference in their lives, but they also bring pleasure to our Father.

Jesus points us in the direction of practicality because when it comes down to it, it's the small things we do for people who are in need that count. We don't have to rack our brains for difficult-to-understand assignments because it only takes us doing little things to demonstrate real love. We do not necessarily have to be in the countries and cities in the 10/40 window to be doing this because there are individuals and families in need here as well. Jesus only asks that we, as a community of believers, notice the needs within our ability to help and take the time to make an effort to meet them. Then we will begin to see the lives of those with whom we share Jesus' love radically transformed.

THEOLOGY OF THE CELL PHONE

by Daniel McIntosh

Then, because so many people were coming and going that they did not even have a chance to eat, he said to them, "Come with me by yourselves to a quiet place and get some rest."

Mark 6:31 NIV

Have you ever sat in a church service, classroom, or quiet meeting when someone's cell phone started ringing at an alarming volume? Embarrassment and scurrying into bags and pockets is normally what follows.

I remember one time in particular when a cell phone was loudly ringing in the middle of a meeting with 150 pastors, but there was no embarrassment and no scurrying. Everybody was distracted and annoyed, yet the phone kept ringing. Even the person up front who was speaking broke in mid-sentence to try to collect his thoughts because of the loud ringing. I believe that everyone was collectively thinking, *whose phone is that?* As it turns out, the ringing phone belonged to my friend who was sitting right next to me, mutually thinking with everyone else, *whose phone is that?* It rang (in a high-pitched ringtone, I might add) four times before he realized it was his phone that was distracting everyone. Needless to say, I was embarrassed just being in the vicinity of the perpetrator.

> Nowadays it is becoming easier and easier to not fully be anywhere.

In order to avoid this embarrassment, one of the monthly church services I attend always starts off with the same routine: They ask everyone to take out their cell phones and turn them off. Lately, I've begun thinking a bit more about the theology of that request. Yes, the primary thought is to avoid those uncomfortable moments, but at the root, it is truly about being fully present during corporate worship.

In the Gospel of Mark, Jesus encourages His busy disciples to come get away and find a quiet place to get some rest. Jesus is helping His followers to see that there is a rhythm to life. He is warning them about burning out and becoming too busy. I would contend that we live in an extremely busy culture where it is too easy to be constantly distracted. We need reminders in our life to help us to live fully present lives.

The request to turn your cell phone off is most importantly about being fully present during a focused time of worship where you are engaging with the living God. If you were to just put your phone on silent during that worship gathering, you could still step out of the room and take a call or take a moment to text a friend, and all of the sudden you are somewhere else. Not fully there. Not fully engaged. Nowadays it is becoming easier and easier to not fully be anywhere, let alone in a focused setting worshiping God.

In the Gospel of Mark, Jesus is showing His followers the importance of not being too busy, and He explains how to get away with God and be fully present. The theology of the cell phone announcement is far less about avoiding the moment of embarrassment in a room full of 150 people, and it is far more about being fully present when you are worshiping.

SECRETS OF THE MAGICIAN— REVEALED!

by Adam Palmer

[The devil] was a murderer from the beginning, not holding to the truth, for there is no truth in him. When he lies, he speaks his native language, for he is a liar and the father of lies.

John 8:44 NIV

You may think this is a little stupid, a little corny, but I've been learning some magic tricks lately.

Since I was a kid, I've always been fascinated with illusions, mainly because I wanted to figure out how they were done. I'd get books from the library showing how to perform magic tricks and I'd teach myself, inevitably forgetting exactly how to do them and blundering when I tried to perform for my parents.

I never really liked the big, flashy, showy magicians—David Copperfield, and what have you. That stuff always looked too fake to me.

But then there's David Blaine. The street magic guy. He walks around in a t-shirt while doing crazy card tricks on the sidewalk. That's the kind of stuff I've always liked. Simple things, up close, right there.

And so I've started learning a few card tricks. I have a friend named Josh, who is actually a performing magician, and he's been kind enough to take me under his wing. He's shown me a few things that only the pros know, so I've been practicing.

We sort of have a system: he shows me a trick, I go home and practice it, and then the next time we meet, I do it for him. Sometimes I do one that I came up with.

The other day we were sitting in a café, when a friend of his approached. Josh hadn't seen his friend in a while, and he asked if he could do a trick. The friend agreed, and Josh commenced.

Here's where I came in: Josh stood up to greet his friend, and while he was doing the trick (which involved giving the other guy some cards, face down), from my seated vantage point I could see the faces of the cards. I had a different perspective than Josh's friend, so when Josh gave the guy a card, I could see exactly which card it was.

The devil plays with a stacked, loaded deck. But it's all tricks.

And then it occurred to me: this is exactly what the devil does to us. The devil is a magnificent showman, and he'd like to convince us of his mightiness and wonderfulness and all around awesomeness. He'd like to convince us that he's the one to worship. That his ways are better.

He is a liar.

He gives us a card of sin and tells us it's really a card of fun. The devil plays with a stacked, loaded deck. He tells us to "pick a card, any card" but really forces his own agenda on us.

He is all smoke and mirrors. He cannot be trusted.

He is not to be messed with.

Look, the devil is our enemy. The Bible tells us that he walks around "like" a roaring lion (1 Pet. 5:8). He isn't really a lion; he just wants to pretend that he is. And he wants us to buy his nonsense.

But it's all tricks. It's all illusions. Sometimes his lies are very convincing, but in the end, they're just lies.

My question for you, for all of us is, are we still playing the devil's games? It's time to stop letting him deal us the cards and call him what he really is—a liar.

"I'M FIVE."

by Jason Jackson

Nothing between us and God, our faces shining with the brightness of his face. And so we are transfigured much like the Messiah, our lives gradually becoming brighter and more beautiful as God enters our lives and we become like him.

2 Corinthians 3:17,18 MESSAGE

May the Master of Life teach us the best way to live and may our lives as students "gradually becoming brighter and more beautiful as God enters our lives and we become like him" (2 Cor. 3:18 MESSAGE).

My best friend and neighbor, Mark, has three children: Morgan, Jackson, and Charlie. They call me "Uncle Jason," and they amaze me. I met Morgan a few months before her first birthday. Now she is a brilliant young lady knocking loudly on the door of adolescence. Jackson is a mini version of Seth Cohen (Adam Brody's character on *The O.C.*) – a lanky lad with amazing hair, an unbelievable imagination, and a fascination with media he inherited from his film-creating father. And then there's Charlie.

Like his older siblings, Charlie possesses a remarkable amount of wit, charm, and intelligence mixed with his unique flair. Charlie recently turned five and, in Steele fashion, we partied well. The "Lego Knight" extravaganza included makeshift costumes with cardboard swords, a knighting ceremony, and a slaying of the dragon piñata (which was preceded by the near slaying of numerous children, who despite parental warnings, continually wandered toward the sword-swinging knights in battle).

As I waited for the dragon to burst with a satchel full of extra candy to add to the bounty, I thought about Charlie before his third birthday. For the few months preceding his gala, the boy was convinced he was five years old already.

"Charlie, how old are you?"

"I'm five!" he screamed brandishing five fingers in the air. If I tried to challenge his conclusion, I was met with a commanding, "NO! I'm five."

Even if I tried to rationalize with him, he only responded more loudly. (Life tip: Never rationalize with a child. Despite popular opinion, they are incapable of understanding deductive reasoning. I'm hoping this comes in handy when I am a parent.) Eventually, Charlie's actual fifth birthday arrived.

I love so many things about kids, but is anything more precious than hearing them talk about their age or their upcoming birthday? Simply alluding to the topic elicits an uninhibited flow of pure joy from most children. Much of that stems from the univer-

> Like a child hoping to become something more, each passing year is accompanied by becoming more like Jesus.

sal love we all have for being the topic of conversation, but there is something else present. Birthdays symbolize growing up, becoming an adult, or becoming more like Mom and Dad, which is the true goal of childhood no matter how vehemently that is denied in adolescence.

I wonder if birthdays are the reason why most Evangelicals place emphasis on recognizing a specific day for new birth in Christ. For me it was March 28, 1995, at Ken Quintus's dining room table that I first encountered (or acknowledged) the living presence of the Messiah. I understand salvation in different ways now then I did then, but there is still something meaningful in that date.

The significance mirrors that of a child's birthday. Of course, there is the personal (i.e. self-centered) element. I know Jesus sacrificed Himself for the world. The date reminds me of my inclusion. Additionally, like a child hoping to become something more, each passing year is accompanied by becoming more like Jesus. As Dallas Willard writes, "I am with Him learning from Him how to be like Him."[1]

To conclude, every March humbles me. In it God gently reminds me that I have a lot to learn—a lot of growing up still to

---

[1] Dallas Willard, *Divine Conspiracy*, (New York: NY, HarperCollins Publisher © 1998), p. 276.

experience. Sometimes the presentation of the message of Jesus causes us to expect radical transformation overnight, but the altering of our souls occurs over a lifetime. Learning to live the way of Christ takes time—a long time in many respects, but my hope is that you will choose to be an attentive student.

Allow God to take all the time He needs to work in you, and don't get so anxious for the end product that you miss the important milestones during your life journey. There's no shame in admitting, "I'm three."

SPEED LIMIT EXPERIMENT

By Daniel McIntosh

> *Submit yourselves for the Lord's sake to every authority instituted among men: whether to the king, as the supreme authority, or to governors, who are sent by him to punish those who do wrong and to commend those who do right.*

1 Peter 2:13,14 NIV

On a road trip, a friend was urging me to do a U-turn as we were seeking to get back on track to our destination, Busch Stadium in St. Louis. I had a "NO U-TURN" sign staring me right in the face, so I opted to take a left, followed by a six-point turnaround in a neighborhood. We were in a hurry, and this led to the questioning of my driving skills (the six-point turnaround wasn't helping my case).

With my skills on the line, I told him it was unethical to do a U-turn when the sign was clearly telling me not to perform such a procedure. He took this as a jab at his principles and retorted by calling out the hypocrisy of my statement because I had been driving five to ten miles per hour over the speed limit the whole way from Tulsa to St. Louis. Rest assured, we are miraculously still friends despite this dispute.

> It is easy to go with the flow because that is the normal trend in culture.

On the way, home, I started a legalistic experiment to obey all of the posted speed limit signs no matter what the cost. As we jumped back onto the highway, it became evident to me that few people follow the posted speed limits on major highways. I felt like I was going at a snail's pace, while everyone else was zooming past me. It was almost laughable. People passing by me would look over in anger as if I was stopped in the middle of the road.

The whole experiment was embarrassing at times, but in the end it was very enlightening. I came away with three major observations. First, going the speed limit takes a lot of submission. I had to practice submitting to an authority over me whose intent is to protect and keep me safe. I had to give up my desire to drive fast and submit to driving at a safer speed. Richard Foster defines submission as "freedom from the everlasting burden of always having to get your own way."[2] This was definitely the case with the speed limit experiment.

Second, very few people were obeying the posted speed limit. I began to make a connection between traffic laws and biblical

---

[2]   Richard J. Foster, *Prayer: Finding the Heart's True Home,* (New York: NY, HarperCollins Publishers © 1992), pg. 54.

law. When everyone around us deems something morally appropriate, it is easy to fit into the cultural norm without giving it much thought. In other words, it is easy to go with the flow because that is the normal trend in culture. The same is true for going ten miles over the speed limit on the highway—it seems so normal. It reminded me of the passage, "But small is the gate and narrow the road that leads to life, and only a few find it" (Matt. 7:14 NIV).

My third observation was that while I was obeying the posted speed limit, I was free from worry. I never got that sinking feeling in my gut that I was going to get pulled over when I saw a police officer with their lights on. I no longer felt the small, remote twinge that I was doing something wrong. I felt free because I didn't have to keep looking over my shoulder.

Submission is about coming underneath God's rule and reign. That's hard. That's demanding. But that's what being a disciple is all about: being counter-cultural in a world that considers the way of God foolishness. Submission is giving up control of our own kingdoms to come underneath the Kingdom of God. The rewards help us find a dependence on our Maker.

THE WHAC-A-MOLE™ PRINCIPLE

by Adam Palmer

Carry each other's burdens, and in this way you will fulfill the law of Christ.

Galatians 6:2 NIV

Raise your hand if you don't know what Whac-A-Mole™ is. Okay, everyone with their hands up, do you have a cave as your home address? Seriously, who *doesn't* know about Whac-A-Mole™, right?

All right, just in case you've never seen or played it (or have and just didn't know the name of the game), it's a game at fairs, carnivals, or pizza-themed restaurants with large, mechanized, rodent mascots. You know the one. There's a big, cushy mallet, a bunch of holes, and a plastic mole pops its head from random holes while you try to use the mallet to whack it. After a little while, the game goes crazy with moles popping up all over the place while you whack feverishly in an effort to keep up. The more moles you whack, the more points you get. Obviously, the creators of Whac-A-Mole™ didn't stray too far from the game's basic premise when they named it.

Sounds a lot like life, no?

Doesn't it seem like we go from crisis to crisis, with very little rest time in between? Doesn't it feel like once we successfully whack one problem, another one pops up in a different place? Soon life just winds up seeming like a big game of mole whacking.

Raise your hand if you can relate. (There should be a lot more hands up this time.)

Here's my thing with Whac-A-Mole™ —my son loves the game. We had his fourth birthday party at one of the aforementioned pizza-themed restaurants, and he kept wanting to play Whac-A-Mole™ over and over again.

Why? Because he could never beat the darn thing.

When all the moles started popping up at the same time, he'd get overwhelmed and just start banging the mallet at random. Sometimes he'd whack a mole, other times he wouldn't. Every time his turn was over, he'd realize he hardly scored any points and would be really bummed.

Life is a game that requires multiple players.

Determined not to let the game get the best of him, my wife, eldest daughter, and I camped around the game. While my son whacked away with the mallet, the rest of us kept our eyes opened for other moles. As soon as they would pop up, one or more of us would just smack it with our open palm, a slightly more painful technique than using the mallet, but one that was very effective.

And what do you know? When we all started helping out, we cleaned house on that game. Tons of points. Over and over.

We won the game. Working together.

See, the thing with life is that, well, it's a little foolish to try to beat the game on your own. Tough as it is to admit, it's true: life is a game that requires multiple players.

We all have to lean on each other.

We have to carry each other's burdens.

We have to whack each other's moles, if you will.

It's the only way to win. If you're trying to win life solo, you're only setting yourself up to lose. If you're sitting back and watching your brother get befuddled at all the moles popping up in his life, you're disobeying the law of Christ.

If you need help, ask for it. If you can give help, offer it.

Keep your eyes open and your mallets handy. Working with your brothers and sisters in Christ, you will wind up a winner.

So will they.

ME, MYSELF, AND I... AND ME

by Daniel McIntosh

Recognizing that my calling had been given by God, James, Peter, and John—the pillars of the church—shook hands with me and Barnabas, assigning us to a ministry to the non-Jews, while they continued to be responsible for reaching out to the Jews. The only additional thing they asked was that we remember the poor, and I was already eager to do that.

Galatians 2:9,10 MESSAGE

Community Outreach. If you are anything like I used to be, those two words when used in this sequence cause your brain to switch into excuse mode. If the outreach director asked me if I was free to help with an upcoming outreach, I would flip through my mental Rolodex™ of excuses to find the proper one that would get me off the hook:

- *I've got a lot of yard work to do.*

- *I have to take my dog to the vet. (If only I had a dog.)*

- *I have to tutor my cousin's friend in Pre-Algebra? Yes, that'll do, I'll use that one.*

I knew I should reach those in need, but I couldn't look past myself to help others.

"Oh, Saturday? I'd love to, but I have to tutor my cousin's friend in Pre-Algebra on Saturday. Yeah, big test on exponents coming up."

The outreach director would reply, "That's okay. Well then, we will hope to see you at next month's outreach."

Phew, that was close!

In Galatians 2:9-10, the pillars of the church remind Paul and Barnabas of the importance of reaching out to the poor. Paul's reaction is awesome. He says that he is "already eager to do that." Paul was eager to help the poor, and his writings encourage us to also continually pray for and help them.

My inclination to use the excuse Rolodex™ didn't exactly scream eagerness. I was not eager the same way Paul and Barnabas were eager. I knew I should reach those in need, but I couldn't look past myself to help others. When I began to examine my selfishness a little bit more, I realized that the reason I didn't want to go to those outreaches wasn't because I didn't have a heart for those in need, it was because those outreaches infringed on "my time."

It was all about me, myself, and I. If I was asked to volunteer at a shelter, I cringed because I already had something in my schedule, something that *I* wanted to do. The actual act of helping the poor in our community or volunteering at a shelter wasn't my hang up. It was fitting it into my schedule.

Then a thought came to me—if I scheduled time in advance to help those in need, I instantly eliminated my biggest objection. My thinking changed. If I planned a couple of hours each Saturday to look for opportunities to do outreach, I would have time set aside each week to help someone move into a new house or rake their lawn. Even if there wasn't a community outreach scheduled that week, I would still designate that time to look for opportunities to serve. I was even open to just driving around looking to help someone change a flat tire on a Saturday afternoon.

Designating this time helps us become eager. It frees us from the need to switch into excuse mode. We begin looking for ways to get plugged into outreach instead of trying to avoid it. If we have scheduled time for outreach, then we rid ourselves of excuses and objections. When opportunities come up for us to participate in an outreach, our hearts will begin to say, "That is the very thing I was eager to do."

END OF YOUR ROPE

by Daniel Mcintosh

Blessed are the poor in spirit,
for theirs is the kingdom of heaven.

Matthew 5:3 NIV

The oxymoronic start to the beatitudes, "Blessed are the poor in spirit, for theirs is the kingdom of heaven," begins Jesus' message of a kingdom that is both here, and yet also not quite here. This is an upside-down kingdom that doesn't make sense in our world, but is, in fact, the truth that we need to be oriented around.

"The poor in spirit" are those who are experiencing heartache, brokenness, financial hardship, death, loss, depression, hurt, weariness, struggle, loneliness. How can those things be good or something that helps us enter the kingdom of heaven?

Eugene Peterson in *The Message* words Matthew 5:3 like this, "You're blessed when you're at the end of your rope. With less of you there is more of God and his rule."

> **When there is less of you, there is more room for God and His rule.**

When you are in the middle of heartache, loss, or depression, it can be the beginning of something truly beautiful. In the midst of these hardships, you can see the need for a Savior. It can mean the beginning of surrender. When there is less of you, there is more room for God and His rule.

The kingdom of heaven is easier to find when you are weak and in need of a Savior, which flips the perspective on struggle. Hardships are beneficial. Weaknesses are good. They allow God to be God. They allow God to be your Savior, and they allow God to use a season of brokenness and hurt to grab hold of your heart.

Later in the Gospel of Matthew, one of four biographies written about Jesus in the Bible, the writer tells a story about a conversation that Jesus had with a rich man:

> Now a man came up to Jesus and asked, "Teacher, what good thing must I do to get eternal life?"
>
> "Why do you ask me about what is good?" Jesus replied. "There is only One who is good. If you want to enter life, obey the commandments."
>
> "Which ones?" the man inquired.
>
> Jesus replied, "Do not murder, do not commit adultery, do not steal, do not give false testimony, honor your father and mother, and 'love your neighbor as yourself.'"
>
> "All these I have kept," the young man said. "What do I still lack?"

Jesus answered, "If you want to be perfect, go, sell your posses-sions and give to the poor, and you will have treasure in heaven. Then come, follow me."

When the young man heard this, he went away sad, because he had great wealth.

Then Jesus said to his disciples, "I tell you the truth, it is hard for a rich man to enter the kingdom of heaven. Again I tell you, it is easier for a camel to go through the eye of a needle than for a rich man to enter the kingdom of God."

Matthew 19:16-24 NIV

Now, I don't believe the reason that Jesus told the rich man to go sell all of his things was to make him poor in spirit. I believe the comment, "I tell you the truth, it is hard for a rich man to enter the kingdom of heaven," is significant to Matthew 5:3 because there has to be need. There has to be a need for Jesus to be your Savior and Redeemer.

When you are rich (spiritually or materially), it is harder to enter the upside-down kingdom that Jesus is bringing. When you have it all, it's easy to be tricked into thinking that you can do it on your own. You don't need God's help. You aren't in need of a Savior to rescue you.

The story of the rich man helps me understand the ironic nature of how the poor in spirit are actually blessed. When you have nowhere else to go, when it seems that nothing else can go wrong, and when you are at the end of your rope, you are right on the doorstep of entering into the kingdom of heaven. You are blessed because that trial could lead you into a new way of life that depends solely upon God. All of the sudden, there is less of you and more room for God.

SELAH

by Daniel McIntosh

Oh, clap your hands, all you peoples!
Shout to God with the voice of triumph!
For the LORD *Most High is awesome;*
He is a great King over all the earth.
He will subdue the peoples under us,
And the nations under our feet.
He will choose our inheritance for us,
The excellence of Jacob whom He loves. Selah

Psalm 47:1-4 NKJV

There is a mysterious word in the Book of Psalms that the writers have a habit of adding into the margins. It's as if the writers are trying to tell us something or give us cues on how to approach the text that we are reading. This word *selah* is a Hebrew note. *Selah* literally means a sacred pause or a holy timeout. The writers include it in the Psalms when the text is so intense that they just need to take a moment. Likewise, we all have had moments of *selah* in our everyday lives, but we just didn't know what to call them.

A few years ago, I took a trip to New Zealand with a couple of friends of mine. We traveled the country by RV, so it was a bit like *Road Rules,* New Zealand style. One of our stops on this adventure was the picturesque Lake Matheson—renowned in all of New Zealand as one of the best locations to take pictures, and made famous as the backdrop to the *Lord of the Rings* movies.

Late that night, we found the campgrounds for Lake Matheson and pulled the RV into a comfortable space. Our game plan for the next day was to wake up while the sun was just rising over the mountains so we could capture the postcard-worthy snowcapped peaks reflecting off of the legendary lake. We set the alarm for 6:00 A.M. and loaded our cameras with film.

The next morning we woke up to the sound of pouring rain. Our flawless pictures would have to wait. By lunchtime, Mother Nature was still beating down on the RV, and we were quickly losing hope. A few more hours rolled by, and the rain didn't look like it was going to show us any mercy. We were left with the decision to stay and possibly waste an entire day in New Zealand waiting for the perfect picture or cut our losses and head to our next destination.

Sometimes life is so beautiful that you can't find words for it, or it's so intense that words don't fit.

All of the sudden, the rain stopped, and the sun came beaming through our windows. We made a break for our cameras, jumped out of the RV, and began taking as many pictures as possible of the lake mirroring the scenic mountains. It took me a moment to realize that framing our mountain view was the most vibrant rainbow stretching from horizon to horizon. Plus, visible just below it, was another faint rainbow. Time stood still while the glowing colors burned into my memory.

The fact that we were on the other side of the world in the southern hemisphere, looking at this famous scenery was momentous enough to tell our proverbial grandkids, but to have a double rainbow splashed across the view took that moment from incredible to magnificent. We had to stop, mouths open, cameras by our sides, and just soak in the beauty. That was our moment of "Ahhhh, *selah*," where we took a sacred pause.

Sometimes life is so beautiful that you can't find words for it, or it's so intense that words don't fit. In those moments take time to stop and reflect; take time for *selah* because when we slow down from the busyness that is life, God can show us something new. In moments of *selah,* God reveals what He is doing in us and through us.

THE RISKIEST LIFESTYLE

by Gyle Smith

A new command I give you: Love one another. As I have loved you, so you must love one another. By this all men will know that you are my disciples, if you love one another.

John 13:34,35 NIV

We love because he first loved us. If anyone says, "I love God," yet hates his brother, he is a liar. For anyone who does not love his brother, whom he has seen, cannot love God, whom he has not seen. And he has given us this command: Whoever loves God must also love his brother.

1 John 4:19-21 NIV

So there I was, thirteen years old, peering into her locker. She was the cute, spunky, blonde-headed girl. My crush. And she had left the door of her locker open and walked away without remembering to close it. Her locker was just a few doors down from mine, so how could I resist? I made an inconspicuous stealth move toward the locker and glanced inside.

What did I expect to find? I don't know. Maybe some secret insight into her heart. Maybe something scratched into the paint that said, "Gyle is cute."

The pace of my heart accelerated as I gazed into this hallowed space, and what I found was something quite different than I had hoped for. Taped on the inside of the locker door was a birthday card, which celebrated what had apparently been a recent event. I cringed wishing I had known earlier.

The card was from a mutual friend. I figured if I read the card, it would almost be like having a conversation between the three of us, right? Why not? As I furtively read through the note scribbled on the card, I came across a sentence that is etched into my psyche to this day.

The three of us (card writer, cute girl, and me) were in a class together—thus the beginning of my crush. I thought the time we spent hanging out in class was going famously. I was funny. She was cute. What could possibly be missing? But the note ended with a phrase that went something like this, "At least next year we won't have to smell Gyle's bad breath anymore. Ha, ha, ha." I felt a warm rush of blood to my face and a cold, dull thud in my heart as embarrassment and disappointment swept over me. And I decided at that moment that I would never look into someone else's locker again.

Yes, that's a true story. And, yes, you should pity me. (Insert sympathetic sigh here.) While it was a painful experience at the time, I get a good chuckle out of it now every time I remember

> ## God doesn't reject me. He doesn't fail me.

it. I can laugh because the stakes weren't very high. A deflated junior-high crush is pretty easily mended. However, many of us have had similar experiences where the stakes were much higher. We extended ourselves, opened our hearts, and offered our love to someone else, only to feel the sting of rejection. Betrayal by a trusted friend. A failed marriage. An estranged sibling. These are experiences that make the act of loving other people feel so utterly risky and, maybe, not quite worth the cost.

I used to think that it was harder to love an invisible God that I couldn't see than it was to love somebody that I could see. That changed when I actually started loving people, and soon I realized how much easier it is to love God.

God doesn't reject me. He doesn't fail me. He doesn't have all of the maddening inconsistencies that my fellow humans possess. When I think about loving God, I am motivated by Jesus' tender attentiveness to children, His story of the compassionate father loving his prodigal son, and His utter act of love on the cross. Because of these things, I find God to be safe to love.

When I think about loving people, it's hard not to remember those bitter moments of rejection or those times when people were so stinkin' unreliable. It hurts. As a defense, I quietly close off my heart so that I can remain safe in my riskless world of quiet times with God avoiding deep relationships with other people. I certainly feel spiritual, and, of course, I'm nice enough to everyone else. So what's wrong with that?

Jesus challenges us with words that are, upon reflection, almost hard to believe. He says that people will know that we're His followers not by our exceptional prayer times, not by our proficient Scripture memory, and not by our spectacular worship services. He says that the primary way that people will know that we love God is by the way we love each other.

How could He ask that? It's almost like He doesn't know how difficult it is to love the inconsistent, inconsiderate, unpredictable people on planet Earth. Or does He?

Jesus called us to the riskiest kind of lifestyle for at least three reasons. First, He knows the risk of loving people better than anyone, ever. It killed Him. Second, He knows that every human on the planet has experienced the pain of failed love. Finally, He knows that a community of people who find a way to fail at love time and time again and yet still keep on trying to get it right will serve as evidence to the world of a true miracle. Something as big as God would have to be among that community.

So, I invite you to join the miracle. Love God by loving other people.

YOU DON'T WANT THAT

by Adam Palmer

"Father, if you are willing, take this cup from me; yet not my will, but yours be done."

Luke 22:42 NIV

I have a few kids. Have I mentioned that before? The total thus far is five: four biological kiddos and an adopted son. The Bible says that kids are "like arrows in the hands of a warrior" and "blessed is the man whose quiver is full of them" (Psalm 127:4,5 NIV).

The question my wife and I have is: exactly how many of these "arrows" is our quiver meant to carry?

Anyway, I've done my share of baby/toddler holding through the years. As a loving, doting father, I've always loved to pick up my children and cuddle them. It started when they were babies and even continues to now, full-fledged kids weighing more than I should probably attempt to dead lift from the floor.

And all my kids have loved it—until Dorothy.

Dorothy is the youngest of my biological children and she's currently in that stage of life some people call the "terrible twos" (and that other people, who are either deceiving themselves or being highly sarcastic, call the "terrific twos"). Naturally, this means that Dorothy is prone to test mom's and dad's limits. Plus, since Dorothy was born a strong-willed child, Dorothy at two is like an exhibition of superhuman strength of will.

The child is bull-headed.

The other day she got in trouble. (I forget what for. Dumping orange juice on the cat? Taking the batteries out of the remote and putting them in her nose? Something like that.) I picked her up to remove her from the situation, and then the darnedest thing happened. She squirmed.

Now, granted, that doesn't seem like such a darned thing, but it just struck me as odd. I'm not the tallest guy in the world, but I'm over six feet, and here was this little creature, less than a third of my height, struggling to break free and plummet a relatively long distance to the floor.

Not wanting my daughter to cast herself floor-ward and put a fresh gash in her head, I instinctively said to her, "Dorothy, Honey, you don't want that."

And then time stopped, and God taught me a lesson.

How many times do I do the exact same thing to God? How many times

I'm bull-headed. We all are.

does God speak to me, tell me to do something, show me the right way to go, reveal His will to me, and I squirm and struggle? How many times do I flirt with sin with God whispering to me all the while, "Adam, Child, you don't want that. You may think you do, but if you get your way, it will only hurt you. Trust Me. I know what I'm doing. I'm your Father. I love you. Follow My will."

And then I remember Jesus, in the garden of Gethsemane, preparing to make the ultimate sacrifice for all of us. He understood. He squirmed and struggled for a bit, but He came to the right conclusion: not My will, but Yours be done.

I'm bull-headed.

We all are.

We all tend to want to do our own thing. Sometimes we struggle against God's firm hand. We all have to put our sin nature down. Every day. Sometimes every minute.

We must learn to trust our Father to carry us, even when we don't want Him to. Why? Because His will is the important one.

RESISTING CULTURAL INFLUENCES

by Adam Palmer

Go out into the world uncorrupted, a breath of fresh air in this squalid and polluted society. Provide people with a glimpse of good living and of the living God. Carry the light-giving Message into the night so I'll have good cause to be proud of you on the day that Christ returns. You'll be living proof that I didn't go to all this work for nothing.

Philippians 2:15-16 MESSAGE

If you met me for the first time in, say, the last eight months, then you might not have known this about me: I am not an athletic person by nature. I spent most of my young formative years with my nose in a book, devouring whatever Narnia adventure or Encyclopedia Brown mystery I could get my hands on.

As a teenager, I enjoyed the occasional game of pick-up basketball or some semi-friendly tackle football in the mud. Even then, I always made sure to get on the team opposite from my

> # You only get stronger through resistance.

friend Alex who was also a lanky brainiac. That way we could guard each other and avoid actual athleticism.

Then adulthood hit and I got married and I had a million children and my metabolism shifted into a lower gear I didn't know existed. Suddenly, I was eating like a teenager but not avoiding the weight associated with said eating. My pants were fitting tighter and actually bursting buttons. (I'm not kidding either. That really happened. Even worse: it happened at church.)

So, a few months ago, I realized that I shouldn't be winded when I got to the top of the stairs. I realized that two bowls of Apple Jacks before bed wasn't a good idea. I realized that I had to get fit. What'd I do? I started exercising. Working out. And I discovered something in the midst of it all:

You only get stronger through resistance.

Every push-up, every pull-up, every sit-up I did involved forcing my body against some sort of resistance, usually its own weight. By pushing against resistance, I tore down the muscle fibers in my body, which then rebuilt themselves over the next few hours. And when they rebuilt themselves, they were a little stronger than they were before I met the resistance.

Resistances makes you stronger.

Our culture assaults us with messages that run counter to the Christian lifestyle: celebrating lust, violence, anarchy, rebellion, selfishness, vanity...the list goes on. And it feels like these cultural influences are unavoidable, until they weigh upon us more heavily than we think we can bear. But, as I learned through my workouts, resisting weight is the way we get stronger. When we resist the life-derailing messages of our culture, we become stronger spiritually. When we resist temptation, we are that much more able to resist it the next time around.

Now, I'm not advocating that we deliberately put ourselves into dangerous positions just to resist them, especially if we have a bent toward a particular sin. If I really struggle with holding up convenience stores, I should probably stick to using my debit card to pay at the pump. There's no sense in putting myself in a situation where I up the failure ante.

Instead we are called to go against society's grain. Paul called it a "squalid and polluted society" and said we're supposed to be a "breath of fresh air." But we can only be a breath of fresh air if our cultural lungs are working. If they peter out when we get to the top of the stairs, we can't impart much fresh air to the world. We have to work them, we have to build them up, and the only way to do that is to resist.

Resistance brings transformation. It works in the physical world, and it works in the spiritual one too. The question is: are we willing to put in the work to resist?

CLIMB OUT OF YOUR COFFIN

by Mark Steele

Don't waste your time on useless work, mere busywork, the barren pursuits of darkness. Expose these things for the sham they are. It's a scandal when people waste their lives on things they must do in the darkness where no one will see. Rip the cover off those frauds and see how attractive they look in the light of Christ.

Wake up from your sleep,

Climb out of your coffins;

Christ will show you the light!

So watch your step. Use your head. Make the most of every chance you get. These are desperate times!

Ephesians 5:11-16 MESSAGE

Have you ever seen an animal play possum? It doesn't have to be an actual possum. Any animal, if frightened enough, can suddenly go limp and seemingly unconscious. The stiffness of rigor mortis, the tongue drooping out of the side of the mouth like a slug all give the appearance that the animal in question is indeed dead. This is a kneejerk reaction many animals have to an impending threat of harm. It is theory that if you make the world outside think you are already too damaged to pound, the beatings will cease.

> **What we pretend is inevitably what we become.**

Isn't this just the way we tend to respond to potential hurt? We shut down, curl up inside our shell, or worse yet, wear that shell in front of a world that has no idea that our life is an extended game of pretending. We wouldn't define it as shallowness as much as we would call it a defense mechanism, but there is an inherent problem in faking it. What we pretend is inevitably what we become. Our cover-ups are meant to be the exception to who we are, but they often end up the rule.

It is easy to play dead. This world hurts. It hurts a lot. And with everything that our lives suffer, it is easy to hide the pain with a façade. We detach. We grow cold. We distance ourselves. We fill our lives with busywork and trivial pursuits—what Paul calls "barren pursuits of darkness." But these pursuits are not simply fruitless. They are fakes. They are red herrings meant to distract us from the actual plan for our lives—the truly fulfilling reality of what could happen if we faced the pain and stopped playing possum.

Paul goes even further to suggest that these fake pursuits are coffins. We believe we have control over our fraud while it is, in fact, slowly burying us. We pray for God to get us out of our situation without realizing that it is a situation we have built ourselves. Thank God we are given the answer.

Here are three steps Paul gives us to climb back into reality:

1. RIP THE COVER OFF – Expose the lies by accepting the truth. The pursuits you cover your pain with are not the real you. Admit it. In the light of God's truth, those pursuits will look like a lie.

2. WAKE UP – Face the music. Moving forward into God's plan for your life may require facing some past or present pain, but without facing it, you are slowly dying. Choose to get real.

3. CLIMB OUT – Take the first step toward healing. Most of the time, climbing out of the coffin requires the help of others to pull you out. Get honest with someone on your church's pastoral staff or an accountability partner about your issues. Then connect and seek God's next steps for your life.

There are too few people in this world being truly and radically reached because there are far too many reachers playing dead. God has called us to face our pain and heal others' pain. But this will not happen until we each stand on our own two feet and refuse to play possum.

CLARIFIED

by Mark Steele

And then he told me,
My grace is enough; it's all you need.
My strength comes into its own in your weakness.
Once I heard that, I was glad to let it happen. I quit focusing on
the handicap and began appreciating the gift.

2 Corinthians 12:8 MESSAGE

Where does this all-consuming need to be perfect come from? It hardly matters how flawed I have proven time and again to actually be—I often feel the weight of guilt for not getting life exactly right. But, this is simply my own perception. God does not expect us to be free from weakness. He does, however, expect us to each do something healthy with the burden we carry. He expects us to use the weight of it to push us into a God-aimed lean so that it's by His strength, not ours, that we carry the burden.

But this realization does not come naturally. Instead, we lean on fear and failure because we are listening for the wrong thing. Yes, we listen to God, but we are trying to listen for the words

> **God has never chosen perfect people to accomplish His plans.**

"you are perfect" instead of listening for what God's voice actually brings.

Clarity.

God's voice provides a clarification that defines our flaws and failings, and then it goes on to describe what our life would look like if we were to lean away from them and into Christ. If Scripture is any indication, God is far more eager to clarify a situation than His followers are willing to listen. For example, before Moses had an inkling to lead, God set a bush on fire. Joseph's God-induced dreams began long before he set foot on the road that would lead him to rule a great nation and cause his brothers to bow before him. The list goes on: Noah and the directions to make a boat, Samuel and a voice from the next room, Saul and a lightning flash that changed the first letter of his name. They heard God's divine clarification for one reason: they were *listening* and not just *presuming* what God's plan would be.

God has never chosen perfect people to accomplish His plans because no perfect person (other than Christ) has ever existed. But, He always chooses people He trusts will actually listen to Him and act upon His words.

This is true humility: an acceptance that we can*not,* combined with a willingness to be the vessels through which He *can.* In truth, it is the closest we will ever come to experiencing perfection: God in us working through us.

In the process, we ourselves become more Christ-like. Not because we achieve or accomplish things out of our own goodness or strength, but because we are open to God's clarification. When He speaks, we listen and respond in obedience to the Voice that knows us better than we could ever know ourselves.

JUST BETWEEN THE TWO OF YOU

by Daniel McIntosh

If your brother sins against you, go and show him his fault, just between the two of you.

Matthew 18:15 NIV

Just between the two of you?

"Just between the two of you" has some pretty massive implications on the content of my conversations, in particular, with the way that I talk about people who are not around (which is just a nice was of saying "when I gossip"). This means no conversation starters that begin with, "Listen to what he did to me…" or "Can you believe how mean/arrogant/overbearing/selfish (insert a sin against you here) that he was tonight?" I have to admit, I enjoy a good conversation starter in which I can air a grievance that I have against someone. It really gives me a sense of superiority, but am I ready for the implications of Jesus' instructions to keep grievances "just between the two of you"?

Let's look at the implications.

In the Gospel of John, Jesus has a prayer for his followers, "My prayer is not for them alone. I pray also for those who will believe in me through their message, that all of them may be one" (John 17:20,21 NIV).

Jesus' prayer to the Father is for His followers to be one, connected, whole. This is a prayer for His followers to be in close-knit communities that would say my stuff is your stuff, when you suffer, I want to enter into that suffering with you, and when you experience blessing, I want to rejoice with you. Jesus' hope is that His followers would be so connected that they would bear each other's burdens. Jesus' prayer is that we would be one.

Now back to Matthew 18, Jesus tells us to go and work it out "just between the two of you." He is assuming that you are close enough with people in your community that you would be able to approach each other and talk about things that have gotten a little weird. That if you have a problem with somebody, you would go to them and work it out instead of finding somebody else and saying, "Can you believe how she treated me?" Keep in mind that you aren't supposed to talk about it with just anyone who will listen to you. It's time to work it out just between the two of you.

This really is about preserving community.

When you share with a friend a grievance you have about someone else, you are bringing another person into the mix, but it should just stay between the two of you. Otherwise, someone else is taking up the grievance that you have with another person, so more people are being brought into the tension. Suddenly it's clear why Jesus says, "Just between the two of you."

This really is about preserving community and about being one with each other. When we don't work it out in the way that Jesus teaches, we start to form groups who get upset with each other. This thing that should have been just been between two people is now causing groups of people to act coldly toward each other.

I have been asking myself the question, "Am I ready for the implications of 'just between the two of us'?" And as I have been chewing on this, a friend came up to me in a local coffee shop and asked, "Hey, is everything okay between us because things have felt a little bit off." It was unbelievable! He was disarming any tension between us and protecting our church community by asking the simple question, "Is everything okay between us?"

Honestly, everything was okay. I was just so encouraged that he chose to keep a possible grievance just between the two of us. He chose, with such a simple question, to keep our community one.

THE ART OF REMEMBERING

by Jason Jackson

*That ye may **remember**, and do all my commandments, and be holy unto your God.*

Numbers 15:40 KJV

For a few summers, I played on a men's softball team with a bunch of guys from church. We were like most slow-pitch, church-league softball teams—all has-beens re-living our grossly exaggerated high school fame. Slow-pitch softball contains the greatest potential for success and the lowest possibility of embarrassment, hence its popularity.

On the last night of our second summer season, I forgot. I was at the game, but I still forgot. I didn't forget my glove or cleats or batting gloves or expressively stylish attire with my trademark knee-high socks and homemade visor, but I still forgot.

None of the details of the game and situation really matter, though some are included for "artistic" purposes. I use that word loosely. Hopefully, I didn't include any unnecessary

> **By my final at-bat, I had developed a severe and potentially fatal case of Alzheimer's.**

details because they are often my cheap attempt at justification, which I am quite adept at, by the way. Justification could be considered my art. Too bad no one buys it.

Anyway, in my first at-bat of the evening, I laced a single into right field that I could have (and should have) stretched into a double. But as I rounded first, I hesitated and decided to head back to first. The right fielder made a quick throw to the first baseman. The ball beat me back to the bag, but I made an amazing play avoiding the tag and arriving safely at first. (I enjoy personal sports reporting.) At least I thought I was safe. The out-of-place umpire with an obstructed view called me out, and I forgot.

As the game progressed, I hit a couple of balls hard but right at the opposing team's fielders. Each time, I forgot again. Each time, I forgot a little more. Later in the game, I committed a fielding error and followed it up by throwing the ball well over the third basemen's head. Of course, I forgot. Between innings, my girlfriend (now wife), Sarah, who was gracious and support-ive enough to sacrifice her time to come watch me play in a slow-pitch softball league, stopped in the dugout to help me remember. Instead of listening, I really forgot. By my final at-bat, a weak pop fly to center to top off my worst game of the season, I had developed a severe and potentially fatal case of Alzheimer's.

I didn't forget everything. In fact, there were a few things I remembered quite remarkably during that game. I recounted the prideful demonstrations and whiny attitudes of my prepubescent years. I recalled the art of subtle under-my-breath cussing and the skills of appropriate argumentation. (*Appropriate argumentation* is the method of disputing obvious acts of athletic injustice in a manner that avoids being ejected by balding men clad in periwinkle blue uniforms.) I retained a level of competition last expressed in high school. Most significantly, I harkened back to the way I treated my ex-girlfriends. I included the definitive "ex" to illustrate the dependable outcome of this behavior.

So, I didn't forget everything…just everything that mattered. I forgot this was a church-league softball game, and I treated it like Game Seven of the World Series. I forgot that whether or not I played well did not matter to Sarah or the team, but only to the insecure little boy inside of me that refuses to grow up and wishes the grossly exaggerated stories of the past were true. I forgot who I was, Whom I was representing, and how to enjoy the game. Most importantly, I forgot Jesus and I forgot eternity and I actually believed (or at least acted as if) a softball game that would not be aired on ESPN had eternal significance.

The lesson I learned is the importance of remembering. A Jewish theologian once said, "to be a Jew is to remember." Studying the Old Testament supports this conclusion. The entire Jewish culture was structured around remembering God. (Look at passages like Numbers 15, Deuteronomy 6 and any passages describing their feasts.) Why? Because we have an amazing propensity to forget.

Think for a second about how many times we have to be reminded about meetings, assignments, birthdays, names, tests, etc. We don't intend to forget...we just do. Unfortunately, we do the same thing with Jesus and His kingdom. A significant part of the Christian life begins with the act of remembrance. In fact, perhaps the art of remembering is more lucrative than all the others.

PARABLE OF THE JALAPENO POPPER

by Gyle Smith

"Are you still so dull?" Jesus asked them. "Don't you see that whatever enters the mouth goes into the stomach and then out of the body? But the things that come out of the mouth come from the heart, and these make a man 'unclean.' For out of the heart come evil thoughts, murder, adultery, sexual immorality, theft, false testimony, slander. These are what make a man 'unclean'; but eating with unwashed hands does not make him 'unclean.'"

Matthew 15:16-20 NIV

The good man brings good things out of the good stored up in his heart, and the evil man brings evil things out of the evil stored up in his heart. For out of the overflow of his heart his mouth speaks.

Luke 6:45 NIV

Okay, so there's this guy I know who is the epitome of rough and tumble, rural, rock 'n' roll, butt-whuppin' Oklahoma. He's got long hair (business in the front, party in the back), black

T-shirts, a southern drawl, and no pity for girly men. I, on the other hand, am manly but more in the software-geek, book-reading, trim-the-hedges, and wash-my-hands-a-lot kind of way. Yeah, that sounds completely weak. But I did play basket-ball, track, and lift weights in high school.

I'm tough.

I am.

Was.

Well, now I'm fat.

In fact, the most physical activity I usually experience is the incredible typing I do in front of a computer 8 to 9 hours a day. I'm suburban man.

So, anyway, this guy and I met at church. We'll call him Billy. He's pretty new to the Christian faith and quite rough around the edges, which is cool. I'm a pastor, and for some odd reason he likes me. He's the kind of guy that tells me "I usually don't like preachers, but I can actually stand you," which makes me feel oddly relevant and even a little tough.

Sort of.

So anyway, after service one Sunday, Billy met me in the sanc-tuary and said that he wanted to get together and talk. I enthusi-astically agreed, and I invited him to give me a call. I have a lot of these kinds of conversations that, honestly, rarely ever turn into anything more. But that wasn't the case with Billy. A few days later, I got a phone call late in the day. It went something like this.

Billy: Pastor, are we gonna get together tonight or what?

Me: Sure. I could probably meet some time around nine. We could meet at Starbucks at 71st and Memorial. Would that work for you?

Billy: Starbucks? What kind of man are you? Drink your coffee with someone else.

Me : (hesitantly) OK. Where would *you* like to meet?

Billy: Texas Roadhouse. We're having steak.

Me: Well, that's really nice, Billy, but I've already eaten dinner. I'm not sure if I could really eat all that much.

Billy (incredulous): Are you kidding? Steak's on me. Meet me there at nine.

And so I met Billy that night, after having already eaten a substantial pasta meal made by my Italian mother-in-law. As Billy and I sat down at our table, I couldn't get out of my head the fact that my stomach was already completely full. As the waitress came to take our orders, Billy of course ordered the largest steak he could find. I, on the other hand, anticipating involuntary vomiting if I ate much more, tried to think quickly of how I could avoid appearing a complete wimp either by eating nothing or by gagging after three bites of steak. I looked quickly through the appetizer menu and I saw something that looked pretty tough: jalapeno poppers—whole jalapeno peppers, stuffed with cheese and bacon, deep-fried. A manlier choice I could not find and so I bravely ordered them. It took me a minute, but I convinced Billy that I couldn't possibly eat anything more than those little fireballs, and he seemed begrudgingly satisfied with my order.

So, we got to talking, and it was really good. This guy was rugged, didn't know all the right spiritual words to say, but he loved God. He really had a passion for Jesus. In fact, in the middle of telling me some stories from his past that made the hair stand up on the back up my neck, I realized I was in the presence of a guy who wanted to follow Jesus with more raw, honest energy than most people I had ever met. He challenged me. Frankly, he humbled me. This guy had a deeper understanding of what it was to follow Jesus than most Christians I knew, and he was definitely not self-conscious about it. He didn't even know he "shouldn't" know this stuff yet. All he knew was the life that he had left and what Jesus had offered him in exchange. And he wanted it.

I wasn't doing any counseling. No advising. I had, without really realizing it, shown up that night thinking I was going to be the expert. Instead this guy was taking me to the woodshed. He was challenging my relationship with Jesus. And so I got completely lost in the conversation. It wasn't until close to the end of the evening that I realized, primarily out of social obligation and some distraction, I had single-handedly eaten all of the jalapeno poppers. All six of them. Did I mention that Billy was supposed to share them with me? Six jalapeno peppers, laden with greasy cheese and bacon, covered in fried batter.

In an instant I felt a wave of panic sweep over me. I like spicy food, and I actually felt pretty good right then, but I knew that this couldn't have been a good decision. Billy, with a smirk and chuckle, also noticed that I had eaten all of them.

So I went home that night, fearing that I had done something very bad to myself. At the same time, I was still reeling mentally from this incredibly challenging experience with a guy whose depth of relationship with Jesus completely surprised me. I had met a true disciple.

And so that night went pretty well. I slept well, no problems. The next morning I did feel a slightly upset stomach but nothing major. I decided to take a few antacid tablets just for good measure and then head on to work. I left for work with a sense of manly power, realizing that I could ingest those little firecrackers with almost no repercussion at all. On the way to work, however, things changed. Slightly.

I felt a twinge. Just a twinge in my stomach that made me think, *It's a good thing I took those tablets.* After another mile of driving, a wave of mild nausea came out of nowhere and then passed as quickly as it had come. It was then that I had the growing suspicion that I might have a problem. I hit the gas (excuse the pun) and sped the car toward work, now fearing that time was growing dangerously short.

My suspicion was correct. Another wave of nausea washed over me, instantly

> Adult man eats jalapeno poppers and wets his pants on the way to work.

producing sweat on my forehead and causing me to double over in pain. It left, and I drove even faster, now knowing that doom was imminent.

And then it happened. A pain filled my stomach that seemed to originate somewhere in my toes and reach its apex right in the middle of my abdomen. For an instant, I was outside of time, in a world where only blinding pain and desperate self-pity exist. So debilitating was it, that I felt like I had momentarily lost control of all of my bodily functions.

No, wait.

Okay, it wasn't just a feeling. I had.

Terrified, I suddenly realized that, in that timeless instant of terrific pain, I had lost control of my bladder. Adult man eats jalapeno poppers and wets his pants on the way to work. Yep, that's me. Powerful, rugged, manly me.

And so I drove with reckless abandon, furiously blowing over the multiple speed-bumps in the parking lot. I parked, jumped out of my car, and swiftly ran into the building in desperate search of the nearest bathroom, which I found, just in time to…well…detox.

Suddenly Jesus' words made a lot of sense to me. What goes into a man will come out was just illustrated with sickening clarity. But this parable of the jalapeno popper has much deeper meaning than just that, because none of us disagree that in the physical realm, if you put bad stuff in, you'll see bad stuff come out. Most of us miss the fact that in Matthew 15:16-20 and Luke 6:45, Jesus is talking about something more. He's talking about something internal, something that is unseen.

The Pharisees and Jesus' disciples were so conscious of what things looked like from the outside (washing hands, rituals, etc.) that they missed the point about what's most important. What's inside of us is what is real, what is authentic, what is truly human in the most beautiful God-created-us way. Billy was a striking example of this. I had all kinds of assessments of Billy based on his appearance and demeanor. But only when I got the chance to hear him, to hear his pain and his passion, did I actually know him. Up until then I had only known an image of Billy that I had constructed in my mind. I didn't actually know him. But when, "out of the overflow of his heart" Billy spoke, did I meet *him*. And it was good. So good that I was humbled and challenged at the same time.

And so in a culture obsessed with image, I challenge you to rebel. Tear down the idols. Crush the graven images, the false identities we construct about ourselves. What would happen if the exterior were the last thing you considered, both about yourself and others? Maybe some of the things you "ingest" might change. Maybe how you invest your free time might change. Maybe some of your friends might change. Maybe some of your life goals might change. Who knows? What goes in comes out, both for you and everybody else. Live like it.

THE CHOSEN

by Jason Jackson

> *How blessed is God! And what a blessing he is! He's the Father of
> our Master, Jesus Christ, and takes us to the high places of blessing
> in him. Long before he laid down earth's foundations, he had us in
> mind, had settled on us as the focus of his love, to be made whole
> and holy by his love. Long, long ago he decided to adopt us into his
> family through Jesus Christ. (What pleasure he took in planning
> this!) He wanted us to enter into the celebration of his lavish gift-
> giving by the hand of his beloved Son.*
>
> Ephesians 1:3-6 MESSAGE

I am generally a confused person. By confused I don't mean
disoriented. I usually know where I am and where I am going. I
just often wonder who I am and how I got here. In college, I
heard the call of the Oracle at Delphi to "know thyself," so I took
a bunch of tests. Personality tests. Spiritual-gift tests. Love-
language tests. Am-I-hot-or-not tests. *Seventeen* magazine tests.
What-should-I-do-with-the-rest-of-my-life tests. And how-
deeply-was-I-scarred-by-my-parents tests. You know the ones. I
think the government secretly mandated everyone take at least
400 of them before the age of thirty.

Honestly, the assessments only deepened my identity's uncertainty. I will never forget taking my first personality test in a room full of other campus leaders during my sophomore year in college. That night I learned that I am a melancholy sanguine, and according to the group facilitator, my personality type is "unhealthy." I'm not really sure what he meant by "unhealthy" or by "melancholy sanguine" for that matter, though, I think I am starting to figure out both.

Of all the labels and evaluations existing, the most confusing assessment for me is quite easy for the majority of humanity to access and understand. I happen to be one of those rare individuals who finds even just *discussing* birth order to be confusing. My wife and her married-with-children friends love discussing birth order. They say things like, "He's exhibiting classic first-born traits," or "That is so like a middle child." They might as well be speaking Swahili.

Why the bewilderment? My mystification with birth order is twofold. One, I have never read or actually seen any books about birth order. Two, even if I discovered that one of these books exists, I would not know which chapter to read because I am a first-born, second-to-last, middle child. I have two adopted brothers who are nine and ten years older than me and I have another brother who is three-and-a-half years younger.

I am convinced that my family of origin is nearly 100 percent responsible for my ongoing identity crisis and accompanying frustration. Looking back on the few years I remember my older brothers living in our house, I realize that I specifically blamed

> **There are so many times that I question whether or not I belong in God's family.**

Brent and Eric for my unidentifiable angst. During a moment of inexhaustible exasperation caused by a fight I was having with my brothers, I unleashed my secret weapon: "You're not even my real brother. You're only adopted!"

If you are adopted or know someone who is, you will quickly recognize the malevolence contained in my comment. Though evil, it worked magnificently. For the first time in my young life, I had the upper hand. I was in control. My brothers stood in shocked silence, equally hurt and appalled. Growing up in foster care and orphanages, my brothers longed for a family in which to belong. I exploited their fear that even though they were finally adopted, this, too, might only be a temporary illusion.

In one of those rare moments of parental perfection, my mother countered, "Jason Randolph Jackson, adoption only means that we chose them. We got stuck with you!" Her words brought instantaneous relief to my brothers, and surprisingly, her words didn't damage me. I knew what her words meant to Brent and Eric, and what they didn't mean to me. Though confused about my place in the birth order, I never questioned whether or not I belonged in the family; they did.

I think about this story often. There are so many times that I question whether or not I belong in God's family. Some days I simply feel out of place because I didn't grow up in church, and so much of it looks and sounds foreign to me. Other days I am profoundly aware of my own depravity and how undeserving I am of any inclusion. In either case, my mom's words now bring the same relief to me as they did to Brent and Eric.

After all, "[God] decided to adopt us into his family through Jesus Christ" (Eph. 1:5 MESSAGE).

A LOVE AFFAIR WITH A PIECE OF FURNITURE

By Adam Palmer

Now you are the body of Christ, and each one of you is a part of it.

1 Corinthians 12:27 NIV

In my lifetime, I have had a total of one awesome furniture find. I wish I could say I've had more, that I'd furnished my entire house with awesome furniture finds, but sadly, I only have the one to my credit (my wife gets the stats on all the other awesome furniture finds).

Ah, but what a find it was. Early in our marriage, my wife and I were at a thrift store looking for whatever we could find, when I saw it: the most hideous chair I think I'd ever seen. You really have to witness it in person to get a good idea of the chair's hideousness, but I'll give you the rundown anyway: forest green velvet; boxy; dark, ugly brown wooden legs; a cigarette burn on the right armrest. Really, words don't do it justice, but they're all we have, so just go with it.

My eyes alighted on the chair, and I decided I had to try it out. Comfort unspeakable. It was like God himself had made this chair, and all its life it'd been searching for me. At last, our souls were united in mutual affection. Once I sank into the chair, I knew that, much like Wayne Campbell's guitar, it had to be mine. Oh yes, it would be mine.

My wife automatically hated the sight of it, but I couldn't let it go, so I convinced her to get it. Twenty bucks later, we finagled it into the backseat of our car, and we were off to our condo.

Naturally, it didn't fit the rudimentary design scheme our living room had, but I didn't care. I loved the chair, and the chair loved me.

But as time passed, my wife began to put her foot down. We moved to a rent house, and the chair went to an unused corner. We bought a house, and the chair went into the garage. She wanted to get rid of it, but I just couldn't let it go, so we compromised. We decided to keep it in the garage where it could remain unused until the day (however far into the future) when I had a room of my own in the house, and then I could move it into there. Basically, as long as she didn't have to look at it, she was fine with it remaining in our possession.

God didn't give me those gifts so I could chuck 'em in my spiritual garage.

Seriously, this chair was the most comfortable thing ever. And it pained me to have that chair just sitting in the garage, doing nothing except hosting spider eggs, but I was determined to keep it, so that's the way it had to be.

The tide turned when I took the chair to my office, only to find my office being moved a month later. I couldn't bear for it to go back into the garage, so I loaned it to my friend Daniel, a bachelor in need of furnishings, who I knew would get some use out of it. Well, Daniel is now in love with the chair and he finds it a magnificent place for reading and studying, which is a must in his chosen occupation of youth pastor.

So, what's the point of my long, rambling story? I often think of that chair as a metaphor for my spiritual gifts. God didn't give me those gifts so I could chuck 'em in my spiritual garage or hide 'em in my office. He gave them to me so I could share with others. That's the whole point of my gifts.

I'm supposed to give them.

And honestly, that's the greatest find of all.

AUTOPILOT

By Daniel McIntosh

And when you pray, do not keep on babbling like pagans, for they think they will be heard because of their many words. Do not be like them, for your Father knows what you need before you ask him.

Matthew 6:7,8 NIV

Right before I walked into an important meeting, I stopped and said a quick prayer. It went something like this, "God, I place this meeting in Your hands." As soon as I prayed that, I noticed a cliché vibe in my conversation with God. Then I thought to myself, *What do I actually mean by that?*

I say that prayer frequently, and the words were beginning to lose their meaning. It's not that "God I place this meeting in Your hands" is a bad prayer, but I just don't think I meant it. It was rehearsed language that I had gotten used to speaking.

In the book of Genesis, the writer tells a story about how a man named Abram leaves his land in Canaan and heads to Egypt because of a famine in the land.

> *As he was about to enter Egypt, he said to his wife Sarai, "I know what a beautiful woman you are. When the Egyptians see you, they will say, 'This is his wife.' Then they will kill me but will let you live. Say you are my sister, so that I will be treated well for your sake and my life will be spared because of you."*
>
> Genesis 12:11-13 NIV

Abram's panic and lies backfire on him and get him into an awkward spot when the Pharaoh decides to take Sarai as his wife.

Years later, Abram's son, Isaac, marries a beautiful woman named Rebekah. Again, there is a famine that sends him to the land of the Philistines, and the Bible tells us,

> *When the men of that place asked him about his wife, he said, "She is my sister," because he was afraid to say, "She is my wife." He thought, "The men of this place might kill me on account of Rebekah, because she is beautiful."*
>
> *When Isaac had been there a long time, Abimelech king of the Philistines looked down from a window and saw Isaac caressing his wife Rebekah. So Abimelech summoned Isaac and said, "She is really your wife! Why did you say, 'She is my sister'?"*
>
> Genesis 26:7-9 NIV

These two stories are amazing. It's as if a script is repeating itself from father to son. Different generations repeating the exact same behavior.

Truthful prayers demand our full attention.

Behaviors get passed down from generation to generation, and this includes things like modes of religious practices, even prayer. Does your prayer time involve following any sort of a script passed down to you, whether good or bad?

There is an aspect of prayer that demands that we are earnest with our words or it can begin to be cloaked in "Christianese." Our prayers can slip into autopilot and become prayers that are full of clichés or words that we don't necessarily mean. Autopilot prayers may sound good, but they don't necessarily have any meaning attached to them. This is where I found myself, walking into this meeting praying something that I wasn't sincere about.

All of that to say, truthful prayers demand our full attention. They demand that you steer clear of being on autopilot while you pray. It means saying what you mean, and being honest in your communication with God. Let's not let our conversations with God become a cliché or a subliminal afterthought. The hope is to be attentive to what we are praying whether in group settings or even by ourselves so that what we pray can be real and truthful instead of church rhetoric. Prayer is simple conversation with God where we retire rehearsed language and replace it with truthful speech.

NOVELTY PROTECTION

by Daniel McIntosh

This is why I speak to them in parables:
"Though seeing, they do not see;
though hearing, they do not hear or understand."

Matthew 13:13 NIV

It has been my experience with warning labels that they are usually correct. For example:

WARNING—Don't take this medicine and operate heavy machinery.

WARNING—Smoking causes lung cancer, heart disease, and emphysema.

WARNING—Dry clean only.

WARNING—Don't iron clothes while they are still on your body.

WARNING—Hot beverages are hot.

Consequently, I am always stunned by the number of warning labels that we, well, that I ignore. For example, after purchasing a Honda Metropolitan scooter (50cc's), a friend of mine gave me a glorious motorcycle helmet to celebrate my new purchase. Now, this was not just any motorcycle helmet (as mentioned before, "glorious"); it was the perfect helmet—a shiny silver, War World II type—for my new bike. For two years I proudly wore this helmet before I realized that there was an important warning label sewn into the inside of the helmet.

WARNING—This is a novelty helmet, not intended for the use of protection.

NOVELTY! Two years I had worn a novelty helmet. At that point, I had a choice: continue wearing the novelty helmet (still *glorious* I might add), or get a helmet that would actually protect me. Adhere to the warning label or ignore it? I had stumbled across the truth about my WWII helmet. It was a phony, "not intended for the use of protection."

In the Gospel of Matthew, Jesus tells a large crowd that had gathered around Him a story about sowing seed. He said,

> *But when the sun came up, the plants were scorched, and they withered because they had no root. Other seed fell among thorns, which grew up and choked the plants. Still other seed fell on good soil, where it produced a crop—a hundred, sixty or thirty times what was sown. He who has ears, let him hear.*

> Matthew 13:6-9 NIV

Jesus is giving a warning to the large crowd. Some of you will hear the truth and still not believe it, "Though seeing, they do not see; though hearing, they do not hear or understand" (Matt. 13:13 NIV).

He goes on to say,

> The one who received the seed that fell on rocky places is the man who hears the word and at once receives it with joy.
>
> But since he has no root, he lasts only a short time. When trouble or persecution comes because of the word, he quickly falls away. The one who received the seed that fell among the thorns is the man who hears the word, but the worries of this life and the deceitfulness of wealth choke it, making it unfruitful. But the one who received the seed that fell on good soil is the man who hears the word and understands it. He produces a crop, yielding a hundred, sixty or thirty times what was sown.
>
> Matthew 13:20-23 NIV

Oftentimes we find truth about God's kingdom, but it gets stolen, doesn't take root, or is choked out by busyness or distraction. It is as if we have read a warning label, received truth from the warning, and then chosen not to abide by the warning. "Though seeing, they do not see."

The devil wants us to continue wearing novelty protection.

In James it says,

> Do not merely listen to the word, and so deceive yourselves. Do what it says. Anyone who listens to the word but does not do what it says is like a man who looks at his

face in a mirror and, after looking at himself, goes away and immediately forgets what he looks like. But the man who looks intently into the perfect law that gives freedom, and continues to do this, not forgetting what he has heard, but doing it—he will be blessed in what he does.

James 1:22-25 NIV

This is about awareness, not guilt, awareness that the enemy wants to choke out any truth of God's kingdom in our lives. The enemy wants to keep us living a lie, even after we have received the truth of God's kingdom. The devil wants us to continue wearing novelty protection even after we have found out that it is not going to protect us. May God's truth find you, and may you protect it with all of your heart, all of your soul, and all of your might.

CUBICAL WORLD

by Daniel McIntosh

I am not saying this because I am in need, for I have learned to be content whatever the circumstances. I know what it is to be in need, and I know what it is to have plenty. I have learned the secret of being content in any and every situation, whether well fed or hungry, whether living in plenty or in want. I can do everything through him who gives me strength.

Philippians 4:11-13 NIV

Usually when I overhear two co-workers having a conversation, I try to tune them out and go about my daily business. But there are some fellow employees who talk so loudly that I feel at liberty to divert myself from my duties and eavesdrop as much as I please. These are the choices you deal with when you work in a cubical world.

To explain myself a bit more, this is the 9-to-5 world. A world where there are TPS reports, mission statements, and electronic organizers dictating your life. Cubical world is boxed in by partitions, which allow you to have your own individual space, computer, stapler, tape dispenser thing, and more, but not necessarily your own office. In this land, the office supplies are plentiful, but you must get your coffee before 9:30 A.M. or else you have to use drinking water to jumpstart your day.

In this office world, I quickly found out that our cubical partitions did not serve as great noise insulators (perhaps because they do not extend all the way to the ceiling), so everything that is said in one cubicle comes in loud and clear to the other hundred cubicles surrounding it. Although you can't see many of your colleagues, you can usually distinguish their voices, and, whether voluntarily or not, you become a fly on the wall of their conversations.

So, back to my co-workers who like to talk loudly. They are always complaining about how great the company used to be. They say things like, "Why can't it be the way it was? It was so great when we used to do it this way, and now it's all so weird and new." They talk about how they don't like the new policies or the new boss implementing the new policies. In fact, they talk about it so much that sometimes it makes me wonder if they ever talk about anything else except how things used to be. Even when they talk to me, the new guy, they love to describe how things used to be before I arrived and how those were the "glory days" of the organization.

> **How much mental energy do we spend trying to change things back to how they were or how we wish they could be?**

Tuning out the drone of their conversations, I began thinking about how much I am guilty of the same habit in my everyday life. I wish things could be different. At times I wish life would go back to the way it was—before a friend or family member moved away. I complain and convince myself that I'd finally be happy if I could just get that new car.

How much mental energy do we spend trying to change things back to how they were or how we wish they could be? When we do this, we are not living in the present. And all the while, life is just passing us by.

Paul writes in Philippians that we should be quite content whatever our circumstances may be. When we are always unsatisfied with our current conditions, life will zoom right past us. If our minds are always preoccupied with the way that life was or the way we wish it could be, then we are never fully present in the now. Our thoughts are either in the past or in the future instead of in the now.

From prison, Paul writes this encouragement on being content. Here he is locked in a cell, fed sporadically, and still he says, "I've learned what it is to be content." When we learn this secret of being content, it allows us to live here and now.

THE "GO-TO" GUY

by Gyle Smith

I am the vine; you are the branches. If a man remains in me and I in him, he will bear much fruit; apart from me you can do nothing.

John 15:5 NIV

Jesus gave them this answer: "I tell you the truth, the Son can do nothing by himself; he can do only what he sees his Father doing, because whatever the Father does the Son also does.

John 5:19 NIV

Did you ever have homeroom class in high school? It was the fifteen-minute class at the beginning of each day where you would hear the school announcements and sit in a classroom with people whose last names were next to yours in the alphabet.

So there I was, spending another morning in homeroom class during my sophomore year of high school. The girl who sat next to me that morning had been in school with me since first grade. We knew each other really well. We had been through every stage of life together, from lunch boxes to pimples. We had maintained a pretty close relationship over the years...a very sister-brother kind of thing.

And so that morning, in the I-just-woke-up-and-shouldn't-have-to-be-here-this-early grogginess of homeroom, I noticed she had a tag hanging off of the bottom of her sweatshirt. It looked sort of like she might have forgotten to pull it off after she bought it. And so, close brother-like friend that I was, I thought that I would be kind enough to help her out. After all, if she saw a stray piece of lint stuck to my shoulder, she would have been considerate enough to brush it off without a word, and I would have received the gesture with nothing more than a knowing nod. So I reached down and quickly yanked the tag.

She and I looked down and stared in disbelief at what I was holding in my hand. It was a bra. Yes, a bra.

My friend, without a word, quickly crammed the bra into her jeans' pocket. We turned away from each other, sat straight up in our seats, looked straight ahead and listened to the homeroom announcements as if nothing had ever happened. I could feel the heat rising up my neck and over my face. Sweat beads formed on my forehead. The last few minutes of homeroom ticked by with excruciating slowness. And as the bell rang, we exited the room into the hallway without saying a word to each other. And neither of us mentioned it again. Ever.

I learned a great lesson that day: Some things are better left alone.

I have a bit of a rescue complex. I want to help people. I see a need, so I want to fill it. I want to be the "go-to" guy. I feel some sense of responsibility for most of the problems I see, so I want to fix them. After all, isn't that what Jesus would do? Shouldn't I take responsibility? While the answer is generally *yes,* it's not that simple. John 15:5 and my life experience have taught me a valuable lesson: I'm not the savior of the world. Jesus is the Savior of the world. And even the Savior of the world didn't fix everything that came His way.

> Just because there is a problem doesn't mean you are the Messiah to save it.

In Acts 3, we see Peter and John going to the temple. They meet a beggar, crippled since birth, who has been there for many years. So long, in fact, everyone in the temple knows who he is. Peter and John pray for him, the guy is healed, and everyone is amazed. But think about this: Jesus went to the temple everyday. For years and years, that very same beggar was at the temple gate every time Jesus walked by. But Jesus never healed him. Why?

John 5:19 says that Jesus only did what He was instructed to do, what He saw the Father doing. Apparently sometimes God waits on things. Apparently, as author Floyd McClung puts it, "the need is not the call." Just because there is a problem doesn't mean you are the Messiah sent to save. In fact, the actual Messiah didn't fix every problem that was presented to Him.

We must be careful to avoid believing we are God. And we must understand that our job is obedience, not rescue. Rescue is the road to exhaustion and frustration. Obedience is the road to fruitfulness. As Jesus says in John 15, apart from Him, from His directives, we can't do anything. But with Him, we can bear fruit. So I challenge you to hear what God is saying about the needs that are presented to you. Listen to hear what God is saying about them so that you can bear fruit instead of bras.

CATS AND COMMANDS

by Jason Jackson

Love the LORD your God with all your heart and with all your soul and with all your strength.

Deuteronomy 6:5 NIV

Love your neighbor as yourself.

Leviticus 19:18 NIV

I hate cats. Sorry if this offends you. My edit-happy English professors warned me about beginning with affronting remarks, but I also hate red ink. I've been studying Creation Theology, which is slowly quelling my loathing, but for now I still hate cats.

I am actually anti-pets in general. My now-wife Sarah and I spent nearly two hours discussing the topic in pre-marriage counseling—our longest session. Cats rest on the summit of my pet revulsion for many reasons beginning with their inherent selfishness. Mostly, I despise cats because of what they do to me.

> **Christianity is too often presented as a series of rules leading toward a narrow and restricted way of life.**

Cats cause my body to experience something similar to nuclear fallout. First, my nose leaks more fluid than my third car, a 1990 Mitsubishi Eclipse. (Don't ask what happened to the first two.) Then my eyes begin to bleed and swell signaling my skin to develop an uncontrollable itch. Finally, the *Exxon Valdez* spills 11 million gallons of crude oil into my lungs making breathing everything but enjoyable and sleep everything but attainable.

Many of us have developed comparable reactions to a word like *command*. We naturally reject its presence, especially in our spiritual journey, for a variety of reasons.

First, we want nothing to do with an angry, controlling, and vindictive God. Because our context for the word is usually negative, we picture a God who commands as either a military drill sergeant yelling at us or a dictatorial parent brandishing a "rod of correction" responding to questions about his or her authority with a swat or a "because I said so." Even as kids we reject the idea of someone commanding us. How many times do we say, "You're not the boss of me"? Christianity is too often presented as a series of rules leading toward a narrow and restricted way of life, but that distorts the true nature of God.

Second, we often associate any teaching about following commands with works-based righteousness. We hear warnings about the dangers of *religion* as opposed to the freedom of *relationship.* Consequently, *command* sounds religious, and we keep far from it. Furthermore, as by-products of the Protestant Reformation, we cling to the beautiful revelation of salvation Paul described in Ephesians 2:8,9 NIV, "For it is by grace you have been saved, through faith—and this not from yourselves, it is the gift of God—not by works, so that no one can boast."

Yet, Paul's next sentence reads, "For we are God's workmanship, created in Christ Jesus to do good works, which God prepared in advance for us to do" (Eph. 2:10 NIV). I wonder if our instinctive response to commands causes us to miss something that Jesus and his Jewish disciples embraced.

In Jewish law or *halakhah,* which literally translates as "the path that one walks," there are 613 commandments or *mitzvot* given in the Torah (the first five books in the Bible) by God to His chosen people. Each command or mitzvah was not seen as a burdensome regulation but a loving revelation from the God who invited them into relationship with Him and gave them His instructions on how to live life in the most beautiful way.

Additionally, they believed that people brought glory to God by obeying His commands in the best possible way and, therefore, doing God's will on earth. The goal of life for devout followers became to *hiddur mitzvah,* which literally means, "beautify God's commands."

According to Jesus, the Scriptures listed at the beginning of this devotion are the two most important commandments. May we beautify God's commands by loving one another.

"I DIDN'T MEAN TO"

by Gyle Smith

You, my brothers, were called to be free. But do not use your freedom to indulge the sinful nature; rather, serve one another in love. The entire law is summed up in a single command: "Love your neighbor as yourself." If you keep on biting and devouring each other, watch out or you will be destroyed by each other.

Galatians 5:13-15 NIV

"I didn't mean to."

I remember saying that to Mom more than once in self-defense while one of my much younger siblings cried in pain from some kind of stunt I had attempted on them. I once lined up every bike and wagon we owned, propped the sandbox cover up on a picnic table as a makeshift ramp, and coerced my six-year-old brother to jump the toys with his bike like Evel Knievel. It actually worked. He soared over every wagon and landed beautifully. But my ideas didn't always work out that way. Like the time I forced that same six-year-old brother, five years younger than me, to box against me wearing wool mittens. I was disappointed to find that there was more crying than boxing.

"I didn't mean to." When I said that phrase to Mom, I wasn't lying. I didn't consciously want to hurt anybody. I just didn't think about the consequences. I was driven by a vision; for example, what would happen if we filled your mouth with as many grapes as humanly possible? But the consequences, particularly those for other people, never entered my mind.

"I didn't mean to," isn't a phrase I used exclusively as a child. Even now, it trickles into my adult vocabulary on occasion. I'm a musician, and over the years I've had the chance to tour with a few bands. Nothing too big, mind you. Just enough to know that touring is little more than sitting in vans and moving heavy things. The music part is less than 5 percent of the experience. Anyway, on one of the tours, our band had the good fortune (or misfortune) of owning a 1969 Silver Eagle touring bus. This was a bus that a church had worn out from overuse and under-maintenance, and it seemed like the perfect vehicle for our world tour (from Oklahoma to West Virginia, that is).

So there we were, a bunch of twenty-something's driving a bus for which none of us had a license and which nobody knew how to maintain. But it was fun. One of the coolest things about the bus was that it had its own restroom. We actually could use the restroom without stopping the bus. Fortunately we at least knew enough to limit our usage to "number one."

We didn't know enough about how to empty the thing to risk being trapped in the bus indefinitely with our own waste. In fact, about a week or two after we first started driving the bus, it occurred to one of us that we had not yet emptied the, hmm, reserve. And because we had been pretty impressed with the novelty of using the restroom without stopping the bus, we had done nothing to curtail our usage of the "loo" (as the British say). So late one night, in the majestic hills of West Virginia, our keyboard player took me to the back of the bus, next to the porta-potty, and explained the situation to me.

"We really need to empty this thing out."

"I know," I agreed. "How?"

"I'm not sure, but I've been wondering what this lever is."

We stared at the black lever near the floor, wondering what it would do should we push it.

"Let's just push it and see what it does."

"No, that can't be good."

"Come on, man! What could happen?"

> The measure of whether we should do something is love.

And so the keyboard player pushed the lever quickly to the floor and let it back up. We looked out the back window and saw nothing. In a determined effort to get results, he stepped on the lever and held it to the ground.

What transpired was almost majestic. A huge white spray twisted and waved behind us like a serpentine offspring of Niagara Falls. Now, finally, here were some results.

What we had failed to remember was our equipment truck. The flashing headlights, honking and swerving, however, quickly reminded us.

We had just emptied all of our urine on our tech crew.

I didn't mean to.

I'm not sure if we ever outgrow the desire to use that explanation, but the writer of this ancient letter to the Christians in Galatia says that these words really aren't ever enough. It's not enough that our intentions were good even though the results were hurtful. The measure of whether we should do something is love. And that love is not just love for ourselves. It's also love for others.

Our culture tells to follow our dreams, achieve the goal, whatever the cost. But what is ridiculously shortsighted about this way of living is that it uses only our own fulfillment as the measure of whether the dream should be followed. If it meets our goals, it is worthwhile. If anyone stands in the way, then he is only an obstacle to be overcome. Unfortunately, many a person has left a wake of hurt and abandoned people behind them in the pursuit of the dream. And sometimes "in the name of Jesus."

In contrast, Jesus tells us that how our actions affect others is the measure of love. He says, "Love your neighbor as yourself" (Luke 10:27 NIV). If your dream will help others, go for it. Or conversely, if it will hurt others, even if it benefits you, don't do it. It's not worth it. It's not God's way of doing things. In short, God is asking us to "mean to." Before launching out into whatever is so important to you, consider others. Jesus did this so thoroughly, that He chose to die rather than continue things as they were. Be like Him.

JUDGE REINHOLD

by Daniel McIntosh

When Jesus came to the region of Caesarea Philippi, he asked his disciples, "Who do people say the Son of Man is?"

They replied, "Some say John the Baptist; others say Elijah; and still others, Jeremiah or one of the prophets."

"But what about you?" he asked. "Who do you say I am?"

Simon Peter answered, "You are the Christ, the Son of the living God."

Matthew 16:13-16 NIV

I find it very hard to act normal when I am around famous people. I get smitten. Some people have the ability to play it cool when they encounter celebrities, but I am not one of those people. I try to play it cool for a little while, but inevitably I get star-struck. I can't stop staring, and that usually leads to asking for an autograph or asking a ridiculous amount of questions that ends up being embarrassing for everybody involved.

Once I was at a Presbyterian church in California when I saw Judge Reinhold. Now Judge Reinhold is not a real judge, but he is the actor who plays Billy Rosewood in the movie *Beverly Hills Cop III*. So during praise and worship, a friend tapped me on the shoulder and said, "Hey isn't that the guy who was in that Eddie Murphy movie?" Immediately I started humming the theme song. It took us awhile to come up with his name, but when it came to us, I began feeling smitten. I tried to listen to the message, but for some reason I kept looking over in his direction thinking about how he shot that rocket launcher backward in *Beverly Hills Cop III* (all the while still humming the theme song in my head).

After church we made our way over to Judge, just to make sure it was him. It soon became clear that I really was standing only a couple of feet away from a movie star. I was star-struck.

We went over to talk to him, and I asked him a couple of incoherent questions about what new movies Eddie Murphy had coming out, or something like that. But I couldn't stop thinking to myself that I was in the presence of someone famous. I talked about that story for the rest of the day, well, okay, for the rest of the week.

Before I tell a friend about my encounter with Judge Reinhold, I usually have to describe to them who he is. I have to explain what he looks like and also refer them to his great display of acting ability in *Beverly Hills Cop III* and his role as the close-talker in *Seinfeld* in order for them to truly understand the magnitude of my brush with fame.

In Matthew 16, Jesus turns to his disciples and says, "But what about you? Who do you say that I am?"

How do you describe Jesus to other people?

Simon Peter answered, "You are the Christ the Son of the living God" (vv. 15,16 NIV). This is how Peter describes who Jesus is to other people.

In order for people to understand our encounters with Jesus, we first have to describe who Jesus is to them. We have to depict His goodness, mercy, justice, faithfulness; and we have to love them so they can have a better understanding of how we encounter the Son of the living God.

"Who do you say I am?" This question is central to the foundation of Christianity. Who do you say Jesus is? How do you describe Jesus to other people? Most people don't know Judge Reinhold, so I have to give impressive details about who he is in order for people to understand our encounter.

Similarly, most people know about Jesus, but they don't actually know who He is, so they need the impressive details. We need to explain who Jesus is in order for people to truly understand the magnitude of His fame. In Psalm 8:9 MESSAGE it says, "Brilliant Lord, your name echoes around the world." Jesus is the most famous One of all. It's an amazing thought that the most famous One of all is concerned with you and me!

EATING AIR

by Gyle Smith

The heart is deceitful above all things and beyond cure. Who can understand it?

"I the LORD search the heart and examine the mind, to reward a man according to his conduct, according to what his deeds deserve."

Jeremiah 17:9,10 NIV

Many are the plans in a man's heart, but it is the LORD's purpose that prevails.

Proverbs 19:21 NIV

The kings of the earth take their stand and the rulers gather together against the LORD and against his Anointed One.

"Let us break their chains," they say, "and throw off their fetters."

The One enthroned in heaven laughs; the Lord scoffs at them.

Psalm 2:2-4 NIV

Self-perception is a tricky thing. So tricky, in fact, that based on these Scriptures, it would appear that any self-perception that is even mildly accurate doesn't actually exist. We think we know how we're doing, but we don't. I can think of a few instances in my life that support this theory. Like when I had this babysitter who was the most beautiful girl I had ever seen. For some reason, I became so self-conscious and rambunctious when she came to watch me that I would run around the house making a chomping motion with my mouth. My explanation was that I was eating air. Somehow, in the indiscernible logic of my young mind, I felt I was impressing, perhaps even wooing, her with my unique and unexpected talent.

Or the time when my friends and I thought we would start a new after-school practice that was both hilarious and daring. We decided to "sneak" into the school bathrooms (it was elementary school, so I doubt there was truly any sneaking going on), flush the urinals, and splash our hands in the running urinal water, spraying it all over the floor and ourselves. Brave and daring we were. And covered in urine.

Or there was the time in first grade when, in reading class, I really had to go to the bathroom. The urge was so bad that I experienced that moment of shame that every elementary school kid dreads. I peed my pants. And so, completely mortified yet determined not to let on that it happened, I reasoned in my mind that if I just covered it up, nobody would ever know. When class was dismissed, I walked down the hall, slapping my hands against my legs. I think I was trying to figure out a way to cover my soaked legs up with my arms while still seeming natural. And I actually thought I was doing it. Needless to say, the teacher called my mom, and, to my everlasting shame, my mom brought a pair of new pants to school.

> **Just when we think we've reached a place of dignity, God sees that we're really just splashing our hands in the urinal.**

We really aren't the best judges of how we present ourselves. And it probably wouldn't be that big of a deal if we weren't so ridiculously arrogant about it. What I mean is that most of us feel the need to appear that we know what we're doing and at times, we actually believe that we do. We say things like, "Don't judge me. Don't mess with me. Don't give me any handouts. I've got things under control. It's my life." But, if the Scriptures are true, and I believe they are, then God is chuckling when He hears us say these things.

He knows the painfully obvious: We have no idea what we're doing. Just when we think we've reached a place of dignity and self-sufficiency, God sees that we're really just splashing our hands in the urinal. Or just when we think we've covered up our failure, He hears our teacher calling our mom to bring dry pants.

There is something really simple that God wants us to know: We're not Him.

The sooner we can figure this out, the happier we will be. It's true, and when we figure it out, we can stop pretending. Pretending takes too much work. It's so hard to appear to have life under control when we really know deep down that "eating air" is the best idea we can come up with.

And so I invite you into what may be perhaps the only truly accurate self-perception you can have: You are not God. It's a lot more fun to live in reality, especially because God created it, and it is good.

IT'S NOT ABOUT YOU

by Daniel McIntosh

They traded the glory of God who holds the whole world in his hands for cheap figurines you can buy at any roadside stand.

Romans 1:23 MESSAGE

The Enlightenment period was an eighteenth-century movement in European and American philosophy. Most believe the Enlightenment period stretched from the early seventeen hundreds and ended at the beginning of the Napoleonic War in 1804. The movement was also closely linked to the Scientific Revolution. Both movements emphasized reason, science, and rationality. Enlightenment thinkers developed systematic thinking, which involved explaining everything. Another major thought in the Enlightenment period was *deism,* which is the belief that God created the world, but then He choose to stand back and watch as life played out: He is not involved in our everyday lives.

Deism thinking and the Scientific Revolution really tried to show that human beings were kings of the universe. Although God was still seen as a major player, many of the thinkers in the age were out to show that human beings are not meant to be dependent upon God. They felt like they could quantify everything through the laws of physics and the celestial realm so that they no longer needed God.

All of this makes me think about a verse in Romans:

> What happened was this: People knew God perfectly well, but when they didn't treat him like God, refusing to worship him, they trivialized themselves into silliness and confusion so that there was neither sense nor direction left in their lives. They pretended to know it all, but were illiterate regarding life. They traded the glory of God who holds the whole world in his hands for cheap figurines you can buy at any roadside stand.
>
> Romans 1:21,22 MESSAGE

The thinkers of this era seemed to have everything figured out. Out of this, the Modern era was born and with it the slogan "It's good to be king." Human beings stood at the top of God's creation, even at the cost of discarding God himself. The birth of technology gave rise to the Industrial Revolution, which stayed consistent with the slogan, "It's all about doing whatever it takes for me to be king," even at the cost of the earth's resources.

We begin to view Christianity and God as a means to get what we want.

The Church during the Modern era predetermined that every believer's ability to work out an individual relationship with God was of primary importance. This idea flourished and resulted in terms we use today like *individual relationship with God* and *personal quiet time.*

Soon people began to present the Gospel as "It's all about you. God can make *your* life prosperous. *You* will flourish with God." This is true, but it only emphasizes the mantra of the Modern era: "It's all about *you.*"

The Enlightenment and the Modern eras were the beginning of a train of thought that is still prevalent today. This is why today life is all about *me:* How can that help *me?* What can you do for *me?* What can God do for *me?*

This is a very dicey philosophy because we begin to view Christianity and God as a means to get what we want. Or we view Christianity as a moral karma: If we jump through all of the right moral hoops, then God will help work everything out for us. He will help us get the perfect job or that Volvo that we have been wanting so badly. In a sense, we have God serving us.

God doesn't serve us. We serve Him.

WATER-BALLOON SIN

By Jason Jackson

At one time I lived without understanding the law. But when I learned the command not to covet, for instance, the power of sin came to life, and I died. So I discovered that the law's commands, which were supposed to bring life, brought spiritual death instead. Sin took advantage of those commands and deceived me; it used the commands to kill me. But still, the law itself is holy, and its commands are holy and right and good.

Romans 7:9-12 NLT

My family used to live across the street from the Garner Golf & Country Club in our small Midwestern Iowa settlement. If I remember correctly, (I have heard the story a countless number of times because it has a permanent place in our family narrative) Thursday night was Men's Night on the course. The parking lot located between our house and the actual clubhouse overflowed with vehicles those nights. My dad normally took advantage of the special evening with his friends, but this particular Thursday evening my parents had other plans.

Mom and Dad decided to leave my older brothers, Brent and Eric, at home unsupervised for the first time ever. I'm not sure what instigated my parents' newfound trust; though I'm sure that at the time my brothers had yet to perform any laudable acts of maturity. Thankfully, they have long since grown up.

Anyway, after my parents left, Brent and Eric called a neighbor friend over to the house. Brent had recently obtained a three-person water-balloon launcher that he was dying to test out. The launcher was basically a huge rubber slingshot that could launch a water balloon up to 600 feet. You would think that watching a balloon travel that distance would contain plenty of entertainment in and of itself, but you would be wrong—at least according to my brothers. Instead of rocketing balloons from our backyard toward the railroad tracks, the boys scaled our house, strategically positioned themselves on the concealed slope of the roof, and began barraging the golf course's clubhouse.

Despite what you might think, slingshots are not entirely accurate, especially when LAUNCHING WATER BALLOONS 600 FEET! It wasn't long before a known family acquaintance who had finished golfing, made his way to his car. Just as the gentleman opened his car door, a water-filled rubber inflatable Scud missile struck the windshield. The balloon detonated and shattered the glass. It did not take long for the shocked golfer to assess the probable origination of the enemy fire. I believe that since he knew my family, it probably decreased the amount of think time required.

I'm not sure how everything went down from there, but I do know that no cops were involved. Punishment included replacing the window, losing the launcher, grounding, and a few more rounds of babysitters. To this day, I think my brothers would say that it was worth it because the story has traveled further than the balloon and created quite a few laughs along the way.

The fascinating thing to me over the years is that water balloons shouldn't and normally don't break windshields. I could take a trip to Wal-Mart this afternoon, buy some cheap balloons, fill them up, throw them at my neighbor's passing vehicles, and the balloons will burst, but the glass will remain intact. I'm sure there would be other consequences like my neighbors refusing to lend me their lawnmower and my wife's disapproving look. The point being that under "normal" conditions, water-filled balloons do not shatter glass. On the other hand, change part of the equation (water-balloon velocity) and another result is likely.

Sometimes I think the same way about sin. I reduce sin to a water-balloon state. Under "normal" conditions, a certain sin is really not that bad. I can do what I know I shouldn't do, and, yes, there might be consequences (if I get caught), but the consequences won't be catastrophic. The truth is, even if I don't get caught, something still breaks. And the more times it happens, the deeper and more damaging the cracks become before they eventually surface.

Unfortunately, for too many it takes disaster for us to recognize sin as sin.

In Romans, Paul writes extensively about sin. At one point in chapter seven, he addresses sin's deceitful nature that leads us toward death. We are so easily swindled into thinking that sin is not that bad (or at least certain sins), and before we know it, things begin to shatter inside and out.

Unfortunately, for too many it takes disaster for us to recognize sin as sin. How many more ruinous moments will it take for us to realize how dangerous water-balloon sins can be? What will it take for us to stop on this side of the wreckage?

WHAT I LEARNED FROM A GUY WHO HAS NOTHING

by Adam Palmer

So if you're serious about living this new resurrection life with Christ, act like it. Pursue the things over which Christ presides. Don't shuffle along, eyes to the ground, absorbed with the things right in front of you. Look up, and be alert to what is going on around Christ—that's where the action is. See things from his perspective.

Colossians 3:1,2 MESSAGE

I had a pastor from a tiny village in Uganda come speak to my church. See, my church supports a lot of different churches/ministries in that nation, so it made sense for him to pay us a visit and sort of return the favor, you know?

Anyway, this guy was awesome. Totally awesome. My wife had just returned from Uganda a few weeks previous, where she'd fallen in love with the African people. This guy's message at our church helped me understand why. The man was full of unbridled sincerity—just this intense, niceness and total absence of fakery.

Amazing.

As I listened to him, I was enraptured with his take on life. He showed slides of his church, which was basically a roof supported by posts around the edges and a few hardwood, backless benches underneath. Another slide pictured the dormitories crammed with cots and old bunk beds, a ramshackle structure made of mason blocks with a corrugated tin roof. More slides showed their kitchen, where each day they make meals for 150 kids. The kitchen was a hovel: four pieces of corrugated tin loosely arranged to make walls, all leaning to one side. No roof. Dirt floor. Two pots full of beans cooking over an open fire. If you've ever seen the movie *Life Is Beautiful,* think of the barracks of the concentration camp and you'll get the idea—only it's worse.

When we saw all these things, we thought, *My, they have it rough there;* probably along the lines of what you're thinking now: *Wow, I can't believe they live like that.*

Yeah, it's true. They don't have it nearly as good as we do.

But then a thought crossed my mind: these people, these African people, don't give a rip about the prosperity message that we hold so dear in the United States.

They are not worried about their own self-esteem.

They do not sit on their hands, fretting about discovering their calling in life.

They are not concerned with finding out their greater purpose.

They do not know the phrase "covenant rights."

They do not shop at Christian bookstores.

> **He cares about living long enough to get to the next day.**

Listen, these things are all easy targets; I know that. I'm making a grander point here, a point about perspective.

You know what that African pastor really truly cares about?

The Gospel.

He cares about *being* Jesus to the people he serves.

He cares about living long enough to get to the next day, grateful that God gave him the day he had.

He has *perspective.* We all could use a little.

During that service, the African pastor shared the following story: The night before he was supposed to speak in our church, he began to worry. He only had one nice shirt and one pair of pants and since he had already worn them that day, they were too dirty to wear on Sunday morning. He told us, "See, I know that to clean them, I have to get them wet, then wait for the sun to shine on them." But it was nighttime, and he was supposed to speak the next day.

Fortunately, he was staying with a host family who simply threw his stuff in the washing machine, then in the dryer. He'd never seen those machines before. Ever. An hour and a half later, his clothes were clean, ready for him to look "smart" (the Ugandan term for "well-dressed") the next day.

You know what he said about that? "If you can make my clothes this smart like that, I know it would be very easy to preach the Gospel."

That's perspective.

KEEP YOUR DISTANCE

by Mark Steele

After three days, leaders went through the camp and gave out orders to the people: "When you see the Covenant-Chest of GOD, your God, carried by the Levitical priests, start moving. Follow it. Make sure you keep a proper distance between you and it, about half a mile—be sure now to keep your distance!—and you'll see clearly the route to take. You've never been on this road before."

Joshua 3:2-5 MESSAGE

We all want to be on the right road toward God's perfect plan for our lives, but we rarely consider the question of distance. Certainly, we understand that there is a distance where we are too far away to be able to see God leading, but Joshua 3 makes it clear that there can also be a distance that is too close. A place where we are so consumed with the promise that we get ahead of the sightlines of an untraveled road.

It is imperative in our lives that we seek God's path and that we are obedient to follow it, but we often cling to the *promise* without embracing the *process*. God does indeed have a plan and

> **If God gave us all the information we wanted, we would attempt to succeed on our own.**

a goal in mind. We often grow impatient, wanting to know the final plan or the big picture prematurely. We become frustrated with the apparent guesswork in the specifics, wishing God would simply scream loud and clear, "This is what will happen, and this is how and when."

God doesn't fulfill that wish because He knows us too well. If we were given the information of God's definitive ending for our lives, in our limited knowledge we would inevitably choose the path that we think would us lead there. But, God's perfect path rarely looks like the one we predict. Before we know it, we would be on the wrong road because we were looking to our goal instead of to our God. When God prepares an unorthodox path, He leads us step by step allowing awareness to provoke us to each new step. If God gave us all the information we wanted, we would attempt to succeed on our own—attempting to impress God rather than obey Him.

This is why God commanded the children of Israel to keep their distance—an appropriate distance. Follow from too far away and they would not be able to see the goal. Follow too closely, and they would not be able to see the journey that would turn them into people who could actually reach their goals.

It is the traveling itself that determines our character, that brings choices and hurdles that define us. If Joseph had not been obedient to serve Potiphar, he would still have been able to interpret dreams, but he would not have become the leader who was equipped to be the answer inside of those dreams. Pharaoh brought Joseph out of prison because it was God's plan, but he named Joseph leader because Joseph had become the right person on the road along the way to God's plan.

Listen for God's voice. Follow. But, keep your distance. A distance that is always alerted to exactly where God is leading next while at the same time taking in every unexpected challenge that refines you along the path.

THE PASSING OF PASSION

by Jason Jackson

Jesus said, "The first in importance is, 'Listen, Israel: The Lord your God is one; so love the Lord God with all your passion and prayer and intelligence and energy.' And here is the second: 'Love others as well as you love yourself.' There is no other commandment that ranks with these."

Mark 12:29-31 MESSAGE

On Monday night, March 6, 2006, I sat motionless on the couch, my unbelieving eyes affixed on my laptop. A single tear formed and gently slid down my cheek. Moments later a few dozen others joined the first on the front of my T-shirt as I continued my stare. Looking back, I am glad I was alone. I know that sounds odd as most of us want to be accompanied in our grief, but this was a different kind of sorrow. These were tears that few, if anyone, in my life would share or understand, though thousands of strangers cried with me. Some (maybe even you) might even consider my emotion silly or even childish, and it was childish in the sense that my sadness was indeed connected to my childhood.

The screen in front of me read, "Twins Hall of Famer Kirby Puckett Dies." Kirby Puckett, one of the greatest baseball players of all-time and my childhood hero, passed away that afternoon due to complications resulting from a stroke at the young age of forty-five. Kirby played centerfield for the Minnesota Twins for twelve years until glaucoma claimed his right eye during spring training in 1996, forcing him into early retirement. Puck was best known for his heroics in Game Six of the 1991 World Series in which he lead the Twins past the Atlanta Braves in seven amazing games.

As a kid growing up in northern Iowa, only two short hours from Minneapolis, I idolized Kirby. I attended numerous games each summer with my family, watched countless more on television, and imitated his every move in my backyard. Nearly every one of his baseball cards found a home in my collection, including his rarest rookie card, which I spent 120 dollars of lawn-mowing money to obtain while in elementary school. His posters and pennants lined my room; his ever-smiling face adorned my T-shirts, and Kirby's legendary defensive acrobatics filled my conversations. I memorized everything about him in hopes of impressing him if we ever met.

My memory failed me, as did my tongue, the day Kirby walked up to me before a Twins game. I stood speechless as he smiled, signed my glove, shook my hand, engaged in small talk with those crowded around me, and moved on to the next autograph. I was

Circumstances change and passion fades— sometimes instantly.

so mesmerized by this short and pudgy yet larger-than-life man that for days I refused to wash the hand he shook.

I met Puck a few more times, each time with increasing astonishment. Though I stopped wearing his T-shirts in junior high for social reasons and I stopped collecting baseball cards for girlfriend reasons, I never stopped loving Kirby. I hoped to be present when he eclipsed 3,000 hits or won another World Series, and I cried when glaucoma stole his sight and my dreams.

Five years later, on August 5, 2001, he was inducted in his first year of eligibility into the Hall of Fame. I watched his speech online. My passion for Puck was rivaled by his passion for the game of baseball.

In the days following his death, his teammates, coaches, and opponents would comment time and again about his enthusiasm, attitude, joy, heart, and, of course, his smile. But just as many people noted that much of that had died in the years before his passing. Kirby's life after baseball was marred in various ways, which seemed to take their toll on his life-loving soul.

It happens to a lot of us. Circumstances change and passion fades—sometimes instantly; other times the death is slow. The Danish philosopher Soren Kierkegaard once wrote, "This

---

[3] Soren Kiekegaard, *The Kiekegaard Reader,* (Malden: MA, Blackwell Publishers, Inc. © 2001), pg. 105.

generation will die not because of sin, but for lack of passion."[3] Is that true for us? Have we become an apathetic generation content with leading lives of quiet desperation marked only by excessive consumption? If so, is that the life Jesus had in mind for us? No, I don't think so.

John described Jesus as the one who came so we can have "real and eternal life, more and better life than they ever dreamed of" (John 10:10 MESSAGE). In the book of Mark we are encouraged to "love the Lord God with all your passion and prayer and intelligence and energy" (Mark 12:30 MESSAGE). Also, the book of Ecclesiastes continually explores the importance of enjoying life.

The interesting thing about passion is, it is often equated with suffering (e.g. the passion of Christ). In other words, to be truly passionate about something, one must be willing to suffer in its pursuit. The problem for many of us is that we are rarely passionate about anything of real value; therefore, when circumstances change, it is easy to let passion slip away. Perhaps it is time for us to move past the passion for fame, possessions, sex, or even success to something actually worth dying for.

DOOR TO DOOR

by Mark Steele

By entering through faith into what God has always wanted to do for us—set us right with him, make us fit for him—we have it all together with God because of our Master Jesus. And that's not all: We throw open our doors to God and discover at the same moment that he has already thrown open his door to us. We find ourselves standing where we always hoped we might stand—out in the wide open spaces of God's grace and glory, standing tall and shouting our praise.

Romans 5: 1-2 MESSAGE

I have three small children. They are not unusually small. They are not carnival freaks. They are simply young, which makes them small. This would not be that big of a deal except for the fact that it has redefined me. I used to be a "creative." Now, because I have small children, I am instead a "minivan owner." My wife Kaysie and I decided that if we were going to own a minivan, we were going to do it right. We were going to purchase the full package: sliding doors that open themselves, DVD screen that lowers out of the ceiling, and a stewardess that roams the aisle. This way, we weren't so much buying a vehicle as we were investing in a second home.

But, there is an inherent problem with having so many features: the features eventually break. The DVD player remote gets lost, the stewardess gets a better offer, and worst of all: the automatic doors stop working. I now have to use an ice scraper to pry the doors open and then throw my body against them so that they slide far enough open to make room for each child to wiggle in sideways. It's kind of like escaping *Poseidon*.

> My doors are blinding me from being able to discover God's wide-open spaces.

I read Paul's words in Romans 5, and I love the thought that God has thrown His doors open wide for me. It is exciting to think that the Creator of everything is that passionate about our relationship, that He doesn't simply "make a path," but He has emotion—great joy and passion—attached to the path making.

But, there is one aspect of what Paul has to say that I don't get too excited about. In order to discover that God has thrown open His doors to me, I first must throw my doors open to Him. Not because God has a you-go-first-or-else-I-won't-do-it attitude, but rather because my doors are blinding me from being able to discover God's wide-open spaces.

Don't get me wrong. I do open my doors to God. It's the "throwing open" part I struggle with. My door engines failed me a long time ago, and now I have to force my entire emotional weight against them just to get them to crack open a sliver. Most days, when it comes to my abilities and effort, I don't feel capable of throwing them open because the doors have grown so heavy.

Behind the house where I grew up on Ethel Avenue was a two-story red brick wall. There were no windows on the first floor which made it a prime candidate for wall sports—you know, dodge ball and one-person bounce-catch. This was in the 1970s, before backyards were the size of a saltine cracker. My brother was throwing a baseball against the wall one fateful day. The pitch went too high and straight into the window. That was expected. What was not expected was what happened after the ball went through.

CRASH!

Not one crash. Two crashes total. When we went upstairs, it was clear that the baseball had, yes, gone straight through the bathroom window—but the real kicker was that the ball also went through a glass shower door.

When I hear Paul's entreaty, I cannot get the image of that shower door out of my mind—a door blown back with such external force that its hinges were literally inverted and the entire door blown to smithereens. God isn't asking me to lean into my door, or open it wide. He asked me to *THROW*, to hurl that sucker open with as much passion as I can muster and as much faith as I will allow Him to give.

The act of opening a door means that the door can soon be closed again. But throwing that door open does something else entirely. It suggests risk, risk that I may do so much damage to the door, it will soon be no longer possible to hide what is on the other side. The hinges will be broken. The door shattered into pieces.

That is why my life, my spiritual life, needs an outside force to give it strength. I do not have enough strength to throw open the door this hard by myself. The outside force of accountability—honesty with the people of God for the purpose of many hands throwing my doors open—is necessary. It is easy for me to jump to the conclusion that there are things God wants me to do that I am too weak to accomplish. It rarely dawns on me that He wants me to do them anyway, but He does not want me to do them alone. There is a reason that wide-open spaces await on the other side of our doors. There needs to be plenty of room because we are not the only ones who are meant to walk through them. We need to pursue strength through honest accountability to our weaknesses. It is then and only then that our doors can be obliterated, never to be sealed shut again.

BENJAMIN

by Jason Jackson

Religion that God our Father accepts as pure and faultless is this: to look after orphans and widows in their distress....

James 1:27 NIV

Over the last couple of years, I have become increasingly involved with social-justice issues. My participation began out of an increasing desire to connect faith and action. Too often we isolate our faith in the private corners of our homes and churches rather than living the teachings of Jesus in the public sector. While attending the Youth Specialties' National Youth Workers Convention a few years ago, I was exposed to World Vision's One Life Revolution program that assists the orphans and widows of AIDS in Africa. It was the perfect opportunity for me to publically connect my faith with action.

My participation has grown over the last few years and led to a significant relationship with the One Life Revolution staff. At the most recent Youth Workers Convention, I skipped the first round of seminars to catch up with my friends and go through their new exhibit called the One Life Experience. The exhibit follows the stories of specific victims of the crisis as participants are guided through an interactive series of stations narrated by the victims' voices on MP3 players. The stories converge at an HIV/AIDS testing clinic where I learned the fate of my storyteller.

Immediately after the clinic, there is a reflection chapel. Pictures of African men, women, and children afflicted by this horrible disease line the four walls. Jesus' parable of the sheep and goats (Matt. 25) graces the front above the altar. Before coming to rest on a pew, I slowly paced around the chapel meeting the eyes of my brothers and sisters in Christ.

And I wept. I've shed tears over the problem in the past, watching World Vision's promotional videos, but this time was different—it was more personal. A few months earlier, I had ventured with a group of short-term missionaries to Jinjia, Uganda. My team worked construction at the Amani Baby Cottage, assisting local craftsmen in building a five-room medical clinic. We spent twelve hours a day, six days a week mixing mortar and laying bricks by hand. If you've never been overseas to work in a third-world country, I highly recommend it.

During our stay, I met a young boy named Benjamin. Benja, a six-year old orphan with a gnarly, however, beautiful smile, had an infectious laugh and a surprisingly large embrace despite his small frame. Being the oldest child in the cottage separated Benjamin from the

Inside this life-full, little boy lives a deadly virus that will someday soon silence his smile.

rest. He spent most days riding his plastic toy bike around our construction site bringing more joy to all of us than I could ever pen. Whenever I broke for lunch, the bathroom, or a drink of water, I stole extra time to be with Benja, as did the rest of my team.

One night after work, our contacts took us for a boat ride on Lake Victoria to the source of the Nile. We insisted that Benja ride along. Benja enjoyed the ride more than any of us, and conversely, we enjoyed him more than the river. At one point, a small wave splashed Benjamin in the face while he was reaching his hand over the side of the boat into the water. He flashed an enormous smile and slipped into a bout of uncontrollable laughter. I stared in the face of one of life's greatest dichotomies. Inside this life-full, little boy lives a deadly virus that will someday soon silence his smile.

Weeping on that wooden pew, I realized that HIV/AIDS now had a name—Benjamin. Before, I was moved by images and ideas, but now there is a person. A little boy in Africa shoplifted my soul and refused to let go. More importantly, Benjamin helped me connect faith and action in the way God always intended. The book of James puts it this way, "Religion that God our Father accepts as pure and faultless is this: to look after orphans and widows in their distress" (James 1:27 NIV).

I wonder if our initial response to commands like this lack what we really need to change. Usually we respond with one-time financial gifts or acts of volunteerism, but maybe we need to go deep enough to connect a face with a name. Maybe we need someone to remind us how pure religion can be when the love of God moves us to action. Maybe we all need a Benjamin, and maybe every Benjamin needs one of us to act.

RESCUING THE LOST

by Mark Steele

Suppose one of you had a hundred sheep and lost one. Wouldn't you leave the ninety-nine in the wilderness and go after the lost one until you found it?

Luke 15:4 MESSAGE

Every winter, I escape for an hour each Wednesday to a tropical paradise. Only, in my paradise, there are smoke monsters, whispered voices, and a band of Others. Yes, every Wednesday, I take a personal retreat to the fantasy world of the television series *Lost*. I love the arc of this story for two reasons: 1) I appreciate a deep mythology; 2) the narrative digs beneath the surface of the characters' lives to discover what has truly made them lost.

This is the irony of the story. Forty-eight individuals survive a plane crash on a mysterious and deserted island—literally lost. But, as the challenges of the island test them one at a time, they each slowly realize that they were deeply lost before they ever crashed.

Many who do not know Christ are in the same boat (or in this case, without one). They know something is askew in their lives, but they have not delved deep enough to understand that they are indeed in need of rescue. They will not come to this realization until their lives face a defining moment. For some, this defining moment is a crisis or disaster—but it does not have to be. In fact, God's mandate to us as His followers is for us to be their defining moment. But, this rarely happens because we do not go searching for the stranded.

> When we live out our faith only on Sundays in a darkened theater, we treat our faith as if we are the island.

Instead, we wait for their crises to trigger the awareness of their own state of being lost—and then we wait even longer for them to figure out where we are seated so they can come find us. This is a double shame. A shame that so many wander for so long without the truth, yes—but also a shame that our lack of movement makes them fumble, search, and beg for rescue.

Rescuing the lost is not something we are meant to attempt casually as it fits into our already-found lives. Rescuing the lost is God's mandate for a healthy, Christ-centered community. When we live out our faith only on Sundays in a darkened theater, we treat our faith as if we are the island—an answer to life's mysteries and miseries that the lost could know if only they would make the effort to stumble upon us.

But we are not the island. We are not even the rescue plane—because the rescue plane doesn't take off until it knows where the lost are stuck. We are, instead, the Coast Guard. The Air Force. We are the ones designed to search the sky and the seas and the mysterious islands and scour the nooks and crannies where the lost do not realize they are marooned. We are not designed to wait for all the details. We are created to be their defining moment.

To find those lost sheep.

To lead them to the Shepherd.

And to reveal that there is a place where they will forever be found.

Prayer of Salvation

God loves you—no matter who you are, no matter what your past. God loves you so much that He gave His one and only begotten Son for you. The Bible tells us "whoever believes in him shall not perish but have eternal life" (John 3:16 NIV). Jesus laid down His life and rose again so that we could spend eternity with Him in heaven and experience His absolute best on earth. If you would like to receive Jesus into your life, say the following prayer out loud and mean it from your heart.

Heavenly Father, I come to You admitting that I am a sinner. Right now, I choose to turn away from sin, and I ask You to cleanse me of all unrighteousness. I believe that Your Son, Jesus, died on the cross to take away my sins. I also believe that He rose again from the dead so that I might be forgiven of my sins and made righteous through faith in Him. I call upon the name of Jesus Christ to be the Savior and Lord of my life. Jesus, I choose to follow You and ask that You fill me with the power of the Holy Spirit. I declare that right now I am a child of God. I am free from sin and full of the righteousness of God. I am saved in Jesus' name. Amen.

If you prayed this prayer to receive Jesus Christ as your Savior for the first time, please contact us on the web at **www.harrisonhouse.com** to receive a free book.

Or you may write to us at

Harrison House
P.O. Box 35035
Tulsa, Oklahoma 74153

About the Contributors

Daniel McIntosh is the youth pastor at Believers Church in Tulsa, Oklahoma, where he fights the systemic abandonment of teenagers in the world. After graduating from Oral Roberts University with a degree in Business Marketing, he did long-term missions work to the countries of Australia and New Zealand. He is an aspiring author and theologian, and he gets from here to there on a Honda Metropolitan scooter.

Mark Steele is a film director, actor, author, and the president and executive creative of Steelehouse Productions where he creates art for business and ministry through the mediums of film, stage, and animation. He has produced, written, and directed film and video projects for clients as diverse as Honda, Purpose Driven, QuikTrip Corporation, Josh McDowell, TV Guide Channel, and John Maxwell. He has also produced and directed some of the largest live youth events in the nation. In July 2005, Relevant Books published Mark's first book of humorous essays, *Flashbang*, which was chosen by Borders bookstores as a 2005 Original Voices selection. He lives in Oklahoma with his wife, Kaysie, and their greatest productions: Morgan, Jackson, and Charlie.

Jason Jackson, his wife Sarah, and their newborn daughter, Cora, live in Wilmore, Kentucky, where Jason serves as the Biblical Hebrew teaching fellow at Asbury Theological Seminary. He is also a teaching pastor for the Offerings community at First United Methodist Church in Lexington. Before completing two master's degrees at ATS, he was the youth pastor at Believers Church in Tulsa, Oklahoma, for eight years.

Adam Palmer is a hardworking freelance writer and missionary to Uganda who has authored or co-authored more than sixteen books. Most notably, Adam worked on *Save Me From Myself,* the *New York Times* best-selling book from former Korn guitarist Brian "Head" Welch. He also co-authored the best-seller *Taming a Liger: Unexpected Spiritual Lessons from Napoleon Dynamite,* as well as *The High School Survival Guide* and the critically-acclaimed novels *Mooch* and *Knuckle Sandwich.* His artistic pursuits also include writing and playing music, which he performs with his wife, Michelle. They have five children.

Gyle Smith is a pastor at Believers Church in Tulsa, Oklahoma. He has written for various devotional journals and served in an editorial capacity for *The Passionate Church* and *The Spirit Driven Church.* In addition, he has worked in Christian film for projects such as *The Passion of the Christ* and *Beyond the Gates* and has helped numerous churches across the U.S. implement evangelism strategies through mass media. While serving as a local pastor he also continues to work in the Christian arts community with artists such as Tribe and Darrell Evans. He is currently pursuing a Ph.D. in Renewal Studies at Regent University. His favorite thing in the world is to be husband to his wife, Kelly, and father to his three children, Sam, Annie, and Charlie.

To contact Believers Church
please write to:

Believers Church
4705 S. Memorial
Tulsa, OK 74145
www.bctulsa.com

*Please include your prayer requests
and comments when you write.*

Fast. Easy.
Convenient.

For the latest Harrison House product information and author news, look no further than your computer. All the details on our powerful, life-changing products are just a click away. New releases, E-mail subscriptions, testimonies, monthly specials—find it all in one place. Visit harrisonhouse.com today!

harrisonhouse

The Harrison House Vision

Proclaiming the truth and the power

Of the Gospel of Jesus Christ

With excellence;

Challenging Christians to

Live victoriously,

Grow spiritually,

Know God intimately.